HOW TO INSURE YOUR POSSESSIONS

THE SILVER LAKE EDITORS

A Step by Step Guide
to Buying the Coverage
You Need at the Prices
You Can Afford
Including Protection for
- Works of Art
- Computer Hardware
- Sports Equipment
- Jewelry and Other Valuables

SILVER LAKE PUBLISHING
LOS ANGELES, CALIFORNIA

T5-AFR-484

How to Insure Your Possessions

First edition, 1999
Copyright © 1999 by Silver Lake Publishing

Silver Lake Publishing
2025 Hyperion Avenue
Los Angeles, California 90027

For a list of other publications or for more
information, please call 1.888.663.3091.
Outside the United States and in Alaska and
Hawaii, please call 1.323.663.3082.

Library of Congress Catalogue Number:
Pending

The Silver Lake Editors
How to Insure Your Possessions
Includes index.
Pages: 226

ISBN: 1-56343-156-4
Printed in the United States of America.

ACKNOWLEDGMENTS

Assembling a book that includes this much information on a subject that's changing every few months is tough. Explaining complex issues in simple terms takes a lot of work.

The Silver Lake Editors who contributed to this book include Megan Thorpe and Christina Schlank. Thanks also to Sander Alvarez, who helped with the early drafts and research.

This is the sixth title in Silver Lake Publishing's series of books on risk and its impact on insurance and other personal finance issues. Other titles in the series include: *Hassle Free Health Coverage*, *How to Insure Your Life* and *How to Insure Your Income*. Because these books are designed to make the concepts and theories of insurance understandable to ordinary consumers, the Silver Lake Editors welcome any feedback. Please fax us at 1.323.663.3084 or call at 1.888.663.3091 during ordinary business hours, Pacific time. More information from Silver Lake Publishing is available on the Internet at www.silverlakepub.com.

James Walsh, Publisher
Los Angeles, California

TABLE OF CONTENTS

Chapter 1
Why You Need to Insure
Your Possessions   **1**

Chapter 2
Homeowners Insurance
Doesn't Cover Everything   **21**

Chapter 3
Renters Insurance Works
in a Few Cases   **37**

Chapter 4
Auto Insurance
Covers Just a Little   **57**

Chapter 5
How Property Floaters Work   **69**

Chapter 6
How Umbrella Coverage
Works   **93**

Chapter 7
How Inland Marine
Insurance Works   **111**

Chapter 8
Specialty and Customized
Insurance   **131**

Chapter 9
Valuing Your Things and
Buying Enough Coverage   155

Chapter 10
Key Definitions   173

Chapter 11
Making Claims   195

Index   221

WHY YOU NEED TO
INSURE YOUR
POSSESSIONS

If they think about the question at all, most people figure the things they own are covered by their homeowners insurance. But people should think about the question more than they do.

Even if you don't own a home, chances are you own other things. You may own a car, a boat, a set of nice golf clubs or a new computer. You *probably* have a bicycle, a stereo or other nice stuff. All of these items, no matter what they cost, are of some importance to you. They have **insurable value**.

> Although the insurance industry of today is dominated by life, home and auto insurance, it's useful to remember that modern insurance got its start protecting people against the loss of things. Three hundred years ago, the informal exchange that became Lloyd's of London began pooling money among English merchants to insure against merchandise being lost at sea.

At various times for various reasons, the things you own might be destroyed—by fire, automobile accident, earthquake, theft...and the list goes on, endlessly. And this doesn't even begin to address the ever-troubling issue of **liability**.

We live in a litigious world. No matter who you are, the wrong mix of circumstances can find you liable—and your nice stuff at risk—if you are found negligent for losses suffered by another person.

For instance: Your neighbor, Mr. Lockhart, strolls over to the house you're renting to return the weed whacker he borrowed last week. Muffy, your normally well-behaved Rottweiler, mistakes Mr. Lockhart for a criminal and bites him on the leg and...er...lower back.

Chances are, Mr. Lockhart won't be so chummy with you anymore. And, having seen all the high-end gardening gear in your garage, he may also decide to sue for the pain and suffering he's had to live through since Muffy's vicious assault.

Liability risk doesn't have to have four legs and German breeding. You're late for work, so you rush out and forget to turn off your iron. A few hours later, your landlord calls to say that fire department investigators have concluded your iron was responsible not only for the fire in your apartment but also the damage to three other units.

The landlord will be upset—but probably not as much as the couple upstairs whose $20,000 collection of vintage jazz recordings was destroyed because your shirt looked wrinkled. If they didn't have insurance on those Charlie Parker LPs, they'll be looking to you for compensation.

Disastrous losses can strike just about anyone at any time. Naturally, these types of risks can be insured against...if you know how to get the right coverage.

> Not only can you purchase insurance to cover your possessions for damage from fire, smoke, vandalism, theft, and freezing, you can also purchase liability coverage which will protect you, your family and even your pet, against claims and suits in the event that you or your property are responsible for damage to others.

Insurance isn't a simple matter. The insurance industry is set up so insurers will profit even when they have to pay claims...but claims eat into these profits. So, even the best insurance companies work hard to avoid paying claims.

Of course, not all insurers are looking to bilk you out of the premiums you pay, but it doesn't hurt to know all the facts before you make an important financial decision such as purchasing insurance.

PROTECTING YOUR PROPERTY

If you own property, there is always the possibility that a **property loss** could occur. A property loss occurs when your property is destroyed, damaged, stolen, lost, or is decreased in value due to the action of a peril.

Property is defined as an item that has a value. For insurance purposes, property falls into two categories: **real property** and **personal property**. Real property includes land and structures built on the land.

All other kinds of property are referred to as personal property or **personal possessions**. This book deals with protecting the second kind of property.

> Personal property can be just about any household item that you, as an owner, find financially valuable—from your favorite CD to your father's prize fishing trophy.

If you were to make a list of all your possessions, the process would be aggrevating and the list would probably be incomplete. To make things easier for both you and your insurance company, personal property is usually divided into several categories:

- dwelling contents;

- high-value property;

- property with intrinsic value;

- business personal property; and

- motor vehicles, watercraft and other mobile property.

Your **dwelling contents** include your furniture, T.V., stereo equipment, appliances, clothing, sports equipment, tools, gardening equipment, groceries, etc. Any items that are usually located in your home are considered contents.

If any of your dwelling contents are worth a considerable amount of money, they may be considered a **high-value property**. High-value property that you may have often includes money, securities, coins, silverware, precious metals, jewelry, gems, watches, furs and firearms.

> If you have a piece of jewelry that has been passed down in your family from generation to generation, you may want separate coverage for it as property with intrinsic value.

If you have property with **intrinsic value**—that is, value that belongs to the essential nature of the thing—make sure that you determine its value when you purchase insurance coverage. Intrinsic value can be a subjective matter. Heated disputes often occur when a policyholder—namely, you—disagrees with an insurance company over a thing's intrinsic value.

To avoid trouble, you may want to have an item with intrinsic value **appraised** before you buy coverage for it. This should prevent conflicts that may arise when it comes time to make a claim. (Appraising your personal possessions will be discussed in further detail in Chapter 11.)

Example: You discover that your framed page of mint 29-cent Elvis stamps was stolen from your office. To you, the stamps were priceless...and, to most collectors, they're probably worth more than face value. But, if you didn't establish their value when you bought your insurance, you could collect as little as $15 (including the price of the frame).

Other items of high intrinsic value include art, records, photography or computer software and media on which data are stored.

A caveat: Most personal property insurance policies exclude coverage for **business personal property**. If you have a computer at home that belongs to your employer, you may be responsible in the event of a loss. (Chapter 7 will go into more detail on coverage for computers.) So, you may want to have additional insurance to cover a business loss exposure.

Property insurance that covers a dwelling and its contents usually offers limited coverage for **mobile property**. This includes off-road recreational motor vehicles and motorcycles, snowmobiles and certain watercraft. These toys are not usually covered by auto insurance. Separate insurance can be purchased for mobile property...and usually *should* be. (It can also pose a serious liability exposure.)

LIABILITY COVERAGE DETAILS

A significant...and little-understood...function of homeowners insurance is to provide a basic level of liability protection. It's the only form of general liability protection that many people have. But even people who don't own homes can face liability exposure. Many standard personal property policies, including what's usually called **renter's insurance**, provide some liability coverage. can provide

> Remember Muffy the Rottweiler? Liability coverage would pick up your legal bills and any damages a court rules that you must pay, up to a predetermined policy limit.

Anyone can sue you—an angry neighbor, the guy who bought your '69 Plymouth, the parents of a kid on the Little League team you coach. If the person suing you wins a judgment in court, you either have to reach a **cash settlement** or face the court placing a **lien** against whatever property you own.

A lawsuit doesn't have to hold up in court to hurt. The cost of hiring an attorney to fight a suit can exceed the amount of the underlying claim. This is another reason liability insurance is valuable—it covers the costs of mounting your **legal defense**.

Which leads to an important question: How much liability coverage do you need? A policy will usually only protect you against liabilities up to the value of the insured property—but most people use their policies as their main protection from civil lawsuits.

> Many property policies pay up to $100,000 each time someone makes a legitimate liability claim against you. If the liability claim against you is more than $100,000, you would have to pay the difference.

So, the issue of how much liability coverage you need has a lot to do with your financial condition—and the insurable value of your property. Higher liability coverage limits are sometimes available—but they can get expensive.

You can also buy stand-alone liability insurance separate from your property insurance. To protect yourself against liability claims that are greater than $100,000, you may want to buy an **umbrella liability policy**. The umbrella policy pays up to a predetermined limit (usually $1 million) for liability claims made against you or your family.

Even if you don't have millions of dollars invested in stocks and bonds, you probably do have some money put away in a **pension fund**. Whether this investment is an individual account—like an IRA or

Keogh—or a group account—like a traditional pension plan, 401(k) or ESOP, it is considered an asset and you should protect it.

> Pension benefits aren't usually exposed to legal judgments. But they have been called into question, occasionally, when calculating damages levied against someone. For this reason, you should probably include pension benefits when calculating your insurable net worth.

In order to decide whether you need high-limit liability insurance, you need to calculate your **insurable net worth**.

Some finacial planners use complex formulas to calculate net worth. But the easiest way to get this number is to add up the **equity value** of any property you own, major personal possessions like jewelry or collectibles and savings or liquid investments.

This calculation can be part of the same process in which you evaluate the insurable value of your possessions. In fact, it's important to think of value of your things and your risk of liability together—personal possessions may be a bigger part of of your net worth than you realize.

WHAT'S WORTH INSURING?

Before determining the type of coverage that you should buy, you need to determine what possessions are of insurable value to you if a loss occurs. This, in turn, leads to an obvious question: What is a loss?

In insurance terms, a **loss** is any reduction in the quality, quantity or value of something.

> Under various insurance policies, loss refers to death, bodily injury, disease, property damage, the physical disappearance of property, lost income, incurred expenses, a reduction in the quality of life (i.e., pain, suffering or handicap) or an obligation to pay for any such loss.

There are some guidelines you can follow to figure out how much insurance you need to cover the loss of your possessions.

One simple way to calculate your insurance needs is to make a list of everything you own that has some insurable value to you—such as furniture (including carpets, drapes, etc.), art or other decorations, appliances, clothes and other possessions. To organize this **inventory**, you simply divide the list into relevant rooms in the house or apartment.

The chart on the pages 10 and 11 should help you review your assets.

For each item, list most recent **comparable value** or **insured value** from other coverages for market value. **Debts and restrictions** include mortgages, liens and other encumbrances on real estate property. They also include margin loans on capital investments and liquidation costs or penalties on accessible pension funds.

> Insured values work best if they include relevant receipts or bills. You should also keep other support documents—including photographs or serial numbers from appliances and electronic equipment—with the inventory.

Household Property Inventory

Property	Foyer or entry area		Living room		Dining room		Kitchen		Bedroom #1 (including closets)		Bedroom #2		Other bedrooms	
	Value		Property	Value	Property	Value	Property	Value	Property	Value	Property	Value	Property	Value
Furniture														
Appliances														
Clothes														
Other														

Property	Bathroom #1 Value	Bathroom #2 Property	Value	Other bathrooms Property	Value	Den or home office Property	Value	Basement Property	Value	Porch or patio Property	Value	Garage Property	Value
Furniture													
Appliances													
Clothes													
Other													

The **total value** of all these things—even if you couldn't raise it by selling everything tomorrow—is what you need to protect.

Once you have an inventory, your insurance agent can help you determine the value of your possessions. The value of possessions will give you an idea of how much property coverage you need.

> If you're not using an insurance agent, the insurance company you're using—or thinking of using—should be able to provide you with historical price ranges for the various kinds of personal property you want to protect.

FINDING COVERAGE

Before you buy insurance for your personal possessions, you should assess coverage you already have.

One place to find coverage for your possessions is under a typical homeowners or dwelling policy. A homeowners policy combines property and liability coverage; a dwelling policy covers only property. In either case, the property coverage is designed primarily for real property.

These kinds of insurance often **don't provide full coverage** for personal possessions; they usually limit coverage to a couple of thousand dollars. And these limits aren't usually enough to replace fine things.

Most policyholders have to purchase additional coverage to insure possessions for their full worth.

> Some policies also provide a limited coverage for works of art, antiques, musical instruments, cameras, sports equipment, and oriental rugs. If you own something that doesn't seem to fit any of the above, you may want to look somewhere other than your homeowners policy for coverage.

However, homeowners and dwelling coverages aren't the only...or even the best...way to insure possessions. And suburban homeowners aren't the only people who need the protection.

Even if you're just renting your first apartment out of school, you may have things that you need to insure—computers, TVs, VCRs, stereo equipment, sports equipment, etc. These things can be worth thousands—or tens of thousands—of dollars.

The **renters policy** is purchased most often by renters of apartments or condominiums who do not require the complete range of coverage provided by the other standard homeowners forms.

If you're lucky, you may also find some coverage under your **auto insurance** policy. However, these possessions must be part of your car—not just items that were stolen from your car. Cellular phones, tapes, CDs, suitcases, purses, golf clubs and any other items you carry around in your car, are not covered under your auto policy unless they are "of" your car.

A caveat: Under an auto policy, coverage is not provided for damage to any property of others that is in your possession. If you borrow a friend's Ming vase for a tea party, accidentally leave it in the driveway and then back over it with your Dodge pick-up, there will be no coverage.

An auto policy also doesn't cover things like radar detectors. Because the purpose of the detectors is to help you avoid obeying the speed limit (and because such equipment has been outlawed in some states), insurance companies won't provide coverage for the devices...under auto policies.

Lastly, some people protect their possessions by purchasing **warranties or customized insurance** policies from manufacturers or retail sellers.

As we will see later in this book, these coverages are usually trouble for two reasons: First, they're often full of exception, exclusions and loopholes; second, they're almost always more expensive per dollar of coverage than blanket insurance purchased for all of your possessions.

ADDITIONAL COVERAGE

If you're starting off with a homeowners or renters insurance policy, you will probably need to look into buying separate, additional coverage for possessions of **high** or **particular value**. In the insurance industry, these additions to a standard policies are called **floaters**.

> A floater is an endorsement tailored to a specific item; the coverage floats with the property wherever it goes.

Floaters can be used to insure a number of particularly valuable possessions, such as jewelry, furs, cameras, computer equipment, musical instruments, silverware, stamps, coins, antiques, paintings, etc. They can be written either as separate policies or as **endorsements**—additions to a standard policy that expand its coverage. (Floaters are discussed in further detail in Chapter 5.)

Whether written for a business or an individual, an **umbrella policy** serves two major functions: it provides **high limits** of coverage to protect against catastrophic losses, and it usually provides **broader** coverage than underlying policies.

Umbrella policies will provide insurance on an **excess** basis, above underlying insurance or **self-insured retention**—a layer of losses absorbed by the insured. (Umbrella policies are discussed in further detail in Chapter 6.)

> The coverage that we have discussed so far has applied mainly to property at a fixed location—your home, your apartment, your car. But you may own property that you either move around or need to transport somewhere—such as an expensive fur coat, camera equipment or a musical instrument. A typical insurance policy won't cover this type of property, or will, at very low limits.

Insurance coverage designed to cover certain kinds of personal property which is not at a fixed location falls into a group of policies known as **marine** or **inland marine insurance**.

While these complicated types of insurance are usually purchased by businesses, some individuals who own a lot of nice things...or a few nice things worth a lot of money...end up using them. (Inland marine coverage is discussed in further detail in Chapter 7.)

You can also purchase **specialty or customized insurance coverage** to insure your valuable possessions. These types if insurance can be purchased on a stand-alone basis or as endorsements to more traditional policies. They include famous odd-ball coverages, like the policies written on tenor Luciano Pavoratti's voice or TV star Mary Hart's legs.

COMMON FLASHPOINTS OF POSSESSIONS COVERAGE

As we've mentioned already—and will see throughout this book—people tend to err in thinking that their basic insurance will protect their unusual assets. Considering this point from another perspective may help illustrate its importance.

Here are just a few kinds of property losses which are **not covered** by standard insurance and therefore, may require you to purchase a customized or specialty policy:

- articles separately described and specifically covered by other insurance;
- animals, birds or fish;
- property of roomers, boarders and other tenants who are not related to an insured person;
- accounts, drawings, paper records, electronic data processing tapes, wires, records, discs, or other software media

containing business data (blank records or media are covered);

- losses caused by the common power failure and ordinance law exclusions;

- losses caused by the neglect of an insured person to use all reasonable means to save and preserve the property;

- any intentional loss arising out of an act committed by, or at the direction of an insured person; and

- losses caused by or resulting from, contributed to, or aggravated by earth movement.

To make sure that you have adequate coverage, pay close attention to the wording of your policy. This applies particularly to the **exclusions** sections of most standard forms.

Here are a few examples, taken from actual policies, which may leave holes in your coverage:

...personal property and structures that are not buildings (e.g., a TV antenna tower) are valued at actual cash value (replacement cost less depreciation) or the necessary cost of repair.

...awnings, carpeting, etc., might be considered as building items but are to be valued at actual cash value and not replacement cost, which is the usual settlement basis for buildings.

Standard types of insurance do not always cover full replacement value of personal possessions. So, be wary of promises or assurances that agents give you about policies that cover **full replacement value**. This term is used freely—but it only applies in a relatively few policies.

> The terms "replacement value" or "full replacement value" usually refer to the structures (house, garage, etc.) covered in a homeowners or dwelling policy. They don't usually apply to the personal property inside the structure.

CONCLUSION

The prosperity of the second half of the twentieth century has had many effects on the people of North America. One of these effects is that people—even those who aren't especially rich—own a lot of expensive things.

You don't have to be Bill Gates to own thousands of dollars worth of computers, stereos, TVs, telephones and sports equipment. And this doesn't even include things like musical equipment, tools, animation cells or other collectibles.

What's the best way to protect this stuff? Should you buy insurance? If so, what kind of insurance should you buy?

The insurance industry has a saying: *The best insurance is the kind that pays when you make a claim.* This is said in ironic half-jest; but it's funny (at least to insurance agents) precisely because it will probably always be a tough thing to maintain.

This is why, to some people, insurance companies seem to change the rules of coverage constantly in order to protect themselves from making payments.

Miscellaneous personal property—the *things* that someone owns—has always been difficult to insure against loss. It's either tough to value accurately or to prove existed at all. So, when it comes to insuring personal property, it is important to **do the detail work** of making inventories and checking specific points of coverage.

After reading this book, you should know how to find the best insurance for your possessions—and how to make sure that it works when you need it.

The next chapter will examine in greater detail the coverage that homeowners, dwelling or renters policies offer for personal possessions.

CHAPTER **2**

HOMEOWNERS INSURANCE DOESN'T COVER EVERYTHING

If you're looking to insure your possessions, the first place you'll usually find the coverage is in your homeowners policy. This is the logical place to start; though it may not provide as much insurance as most people think it does.

The standard homeowners policy is a **package policy**. This means that several coverages—property, liability and certain others—are combined together in a single agreement.

The standard homeowners policy is divided into the following parts:

- Section one of the policy provides property coverage and includes coverage for your dwelling (house), other structures at the same location, contents or **personal property** (in the dwelling or away from the dwelling), rental value of a covered property (the lost income that results when there is damage to property owned, but not rented to others), and additional living expenses (incurred when a covered loss occurs).

- Section two of the policy provides coverage for liability and includes coverage for liability loss exposures, medical payments coverage, and additional coverages for claims expenses, first aid and damage to the property of others.

If you are insuring personal possessions, chances are you won't want a dwelling policy, in most cases, your liability or personal property insurance needs will be better covered under a standard homeowners insurance package.

A **dwelling policy** is similar to a standard homeowners policy. Many of the coverages and the basic limits of insurance are often identical. However, a dwelling policy is designed specifically to cover a dwelling and the personal property in it. The dwelling policy offers no liability coverage.

Dwelling coverage is appealing to some people because it provides the flexibility to include only real property coverage (coverage for land and structures built on the land).

Note: If, for some reason, you don't want to purchase a homeowners policy (you are insuring a second home, such as a cabin in the mountains that you visit only rarely), you can purchase add-on liability coverage in addition to a dwelling policy.

For both homeowners and dwelling policies, an important step is distinguishing who is—and is not—

covered. Generally, because the dwelling package doesn't include liability coverage, its coverage extends to fewer people.

If personal property is insured, the **named insured** and all members of his or her family residing at the described location, are covered for property which they own or use. The personal property of **guests** and servants may be covered at the request of the named insured.

> If the named insured dies, coverage continues for his or her legal representatives. Until a legal representative is appointed, a temporary custodian of the estate would also be covered.

Dwelling policies tend to have a lot of exclusions. Here are some common restrictions on the property covered by a dwelling policy:

- articles separately described and specifically insured in this or other insurance;

- animals, birds or fish; and

- motor vehicles or all other motorized land conveyances. (This includes their equipment and accessories, or electronic apparatus that is designed to be operated solely by use of the power from the electrical system of motor vehicles or all other motorized land conveyances. Electronic apparatus are accessories or antennas, tapes, wires, records, discs or other media used with any electronic apparatus.)

WHAT YOUR INSURER WILL PAY FOR UNDER YOUR POLICY

There are six types of homeowners insurance policies. However, not every insurer will offer all six and the names and limits of these coverages may vary from company to company. But, the following six are the standard types of coverage:

- **HO-1.** The **basic** homeowners policy protects your home against 11 named perils. However, this coverage is rarely enough, so many states are phasing out this type of coverage.

- **HO-2.** The **broad** homeowners policy covers your home against 17 named perils. A variation of HO-2 is available to most mobile home owners. This type of policy generally costs five to ten percent more than the HO-1 policy.

- **HO-3.** The **special** homeowners policy protects your home against all perils except those specifically excluded by the contract. It typically costs 10 to 15 percent more than the HO-1 policy.

  Sometimes a company will offer a **guaranteed replacement-cost policy**. This policy goes a step further than the standard HO-3 policy in that it offers to pay the full amount needed to replace your home and its contents—even if that exceeds the policy limit.

- **HO-4.** The **renters** policy generally protects the possessions of tenants in a house or apartment against named perils. It also provides liability coverage but doesn't protect the actual dwelling, which should be covered under the landlord's policy. (Renters who don't want to pay for liability protection can opt for a policy that covers only personal property.)

- **HO-6.** The policy for **co-op and condominium owners** provides coverage for liability and personal property, much like HO-4. While insurance purchased by the co-op or condominium association covers much of the actual dwelling, individual owners who want coverage for improvements to their units must write them into an HO-6 policy. If you add a porch, for instance, you'll need an endorsement (an addition to your policy that expands its coverage).

- **HO-8.** Primarily for **older homes**, this policy offers coverage for the same perils as the HO-1, but insures the house only for repair costs or its actual cash value, not its **replacement cost**.

Each policy form is designed to serve different insurance needs. **Property insurance** for the residence and its contents is provided by HO-1, HO-2, and HO-3. However, HO-4 and HO-6 do not provide any major types of property insurance for the residence. All policies provide liability insurance and require minimum amounts of coverage.

Typically, your insurer will have **limits** on the amount of coverage that it offers for your personal property under a homeowners policy. These are called **limits of liability**. The limit for each numbered category below is the total limit for each loss for all property in that category:

1. $200 on money, bank notes, bullion, gold other than goldware, silver other than silverware, platinum, coins and medals;

2. $1000 on securities, accounts, deeds, evidences of debt, letters of credit, notes other than bank notes, manuscripts, personal records, passports, tickets and stamps (this dollar limit applies to these categories regardless of the medium such as paper or computer software on which the material exists).

   (This limit also includes the cost to research, replace, or restore the information from the lost or damaged material.)

3. $1000 on watercraft, including their trailers, furnishings, equipment, and outboard engines or motors;

4. $1000 on trailers not used with watercraft;

5. $1000 for loss by theft of jewelry, watches, furs, precious and semi-precious stones;

6. $2000 for loss by theft of firearms and related equipment;

7. $2500 for loss by theft of silverware, silver-plated ware, goldware, gold-plated ware, and pewterware (this includes flatware, tea sets, trays, and trophies made of or including silver, gold, or pewter).

A caveat: Items 5, 6 and 7 apply to theft only. The other limitations apply to all perils. Broader coverage can be purchased on several of these items (e.g., boats, jewelry, silverware, guns), through **floater policies** or other kinds of endorsements but a less expensive alternative is to simply purchase higher limits where the limits above are not adequate.

8. $2500 on property on the "residence premises," used at any time or in any manner for any "business" purpose;

9. $250 on property away from the "residence premises," used at any time or in any manner for any "business" purpose. (This limit does not apply to loss to adaptable electronic apparatus as described in special limits 10 and 11 below.)

These liability limits are not additional amounts of insurance but caps on the total amount an insurance company has to pay for loss or damage to the property described.

---

10. $1000 for loss to electronic apparatus, while in or upon a motor vehicle or other motorized land conveyance, if the electronic apparatus is equipped to be operated by power from the electrical system of the vehicle while retaining its capability of being operated by other sources of power. Electronic apparatus includes:

   a. accessories or antennas; or
   b. tapes, wires, records, discs or other media.

11. $1000 for loss to electronic apparatus, while not in or upon a motor vehicle or other motorized land conveyance, if the electronic apparatus:

    a. is equipped to be operated by power from the electrical system of the vehicle or conveyance while retaining its capability of being operated by other sources of power;

    b. is away from the "residence premises"; and

    c. is used at any time or in any manner for any "business" purpose.

Electronic apparatus includes:

    a. accessories and antennas; or

    b. tapes, wires, records, discs or other media.

Items 8, 9, 10 and 11 have become more important since the 1980s, because so many homes now include substantial **electronic assets**—computers, stereos and video equipment.

Items 10 and 11 offer limited coverage for portable electronic apparatus used in autos that can also be operated from other power sources. Electronic items such as lap top computers, car telephones, compact disc players, and their antennas, tapes, wires, etc., are included in this description.

There is no coverage for electronic items that are permanently installed in vehicles (they may be insured under an automobile policy).

Item 10 limits coverage to $1,000 for the equipment while it is in a motor vehicle whether or not the vehicle is located at the residence premises.

WHO IS AN INSURED?

A homeowners policy can be issued to you if you are eligible, and if you qualify as any of the following:

- an owner-occupant of a dwelling;

- the intended owner-occupant of a dwelling under construction;

- one co-owner of a duplex, when each portion of the duplex is occupied by separate co-owners;

- a purchaser-occupant, when the seller retains title under an installment contract until payments are completed; and

- an occupant living in a dwelling under a life estate arrangement.

HOMEOWNERS COVERAGE

The most widely used homeowners insurance policy is the **HO-3 policy**. For this reason we will use the HO-3 policy throughout this chapter to discuss property insurance coverages.

A typical homeowners insurance policy consists of five types of coverage:

- Coverage A—Dwelling

- Coverage B—Other Structures

- Coverage C—Personal Property

- Coverage D—Loss of Use

- Additional Coverages

Dwelling coverage is the most significant coverage of a homeowners policy. (Except the HO-4 and HO-6 policies). This coverage applies to the dwelling, attached structures, and materials and supplies on or adjacent to the residence premises for use in the construction, alteration or repair of the dwelling or other structures.

Dwelling coverage is also sold as a stand-alone policy (without the liability coverage that the HO-3 has).

When insuring personal property, the most important coverage offered by a homeowners policy is **personal property coverage.** Personal property coverage is included on all homeowners forms. On all forms except HO-4 and HO-6, the coverage is usually an additional amount of insurance equal to 50 percent of the amount written on the dwelling. This limit may be increased or decreased (but not below 40 percent of the amount of the dwelling coverage) by endorsement.

On forms HO-4 and HO-6, personal property coverage is the major form of property insurance. The minimum amount of coverage is usually about $6,000, but the policy may be written for any **higher amount**.

Note: Property coverage on a homeowners policy is broader than it is on the dwelling forms. The full limit applies to personal property owned or used by you while it is anywhere in the world (on dwelling forms, only 10 percent of the limit applies worldwide).

At your request, **personal property owned by others** may be covered while it is on your premises, and personal property of a guest or residence employee also may be covered while it is at your house.

Coverage for personal property usually kept at a **residence other than your house** is limited to the larger of $1,000 or 10 percent of the structure limit. But, if the property is moved to a newly acquired principal residence, this limitation does not apply during the first 30 days after the property is moved.

If, after a fire or other loss for which you are covered under your policy, you cannot live in your residence or use your personal property, **loss of use expenses** such as renting a hotel room, or other temporary housing, as well as the expense of eating in restaurants can be recovered under Coverage D.

> Under this coverage, a combination of additional living expense and fair rental value are used to combine coverage for an indirect loss—due to the loss of use of the covered property.

When a loss that is covered under your homeowners policy makes the part of the residence premises where you reside unfit to live in, you are entitled to **additional living expense coverage**.

Your homeowners policy can also cover some of your personal possessions for a number of additional coverages. **Additional coverages** involve losses or kinds of property damage which are not specifically provided for elsewhere in a homeowners policy. Some of these include:

- debris removal;
- reasonable repairs;
- trees, shrubs and other plants;
- fire department service charge;

- property removed;
- credit card, fund transfer, forgery and counterfeit money.

If you have a tree that was damaged by wind-storm or hail, the weight of ice, snow or sleet, or due to a neighbor's tree that was damaged by any of these perils, you can find coverage under your homeowners policy.

CLEANING UP AFTER A LOSS

After a major loss, debris such as charred lumber, burned furniture, ashes and broken glass must be removed. **Debris removal** is, surprisingly, a common point of dispute between insurance companies and insureds.

The major property coverages of your homeowners policy will pay for the loss or damage, but it will not always pay the additional expenses to remove debris. But, insurance companies will pay a reasonable expense for the removal of:

debris of covered property if a peril insured against that applies to the damaged property causes the loss; or

ash, dust, or particles from a volcanic eruption that has caused direct loss to a building or property contained in a building.

These costs are included in the claim amount as long as there is sufficient coverage to pay for the damaged property plus debris removal. If combined loss exceeds the policy limit, then an additional amount of coverage equal to five percent of the limit of liability will be made available for debris removal.

Expenses involved in the removal of trees that have damaged an insured structure are covered up to a limit of $500 per loss—not per tree.

In addition, your trees, shrubs and other plants or lawns on the **residence premises,** are covered for loss caused by fire or lightning, explosion, riot or civil commotion, aircraft, vehicles not owned or operated by a resident of the "residence premises," vandalism, malicious mischief or theft.

Again, insurance companies will pay up to five percent of the limit of liability that applies to the dwelling for all trees, shrubs, plants or lawns. No more than $500 of this limit will be available for any one tree, shrub or plant.

> **This coverage does not apply to property that you have grown for "business" purposes.**

CREDIT CARD COVERAGE

Homeowners insurance may also cover lost or stolen credit cards and fund transfer cards. It will also cover you for losses due to forgery and counterfeit money.

Your insurance company will usually pay up to $500 for losses related to:

- your legal obligation to pay because of the theft or unauthorized use of credit cards issued to, or registered in an "insured's" name;

- loss resulting from theft or unauthorized use of a fund transfer card used for deposit, withdrawal or transfer of funds, issued to or registered in your name;

- loss caused by forgery or alteration of any check or negotiable instrument; and

- loss through acceptance in good faith of counterfeit United States or Canadian paper currency.

Generally, your insurance company will not cover use of a credit card or fund transfer card:

a. by a resident of your household;

b. by a person who has been entrusted with either type of card; or

c. if you have not complied with all terms and conditions under which the cards are issued, such as exceeding the credit limit of the card.

Losses resulting from a series of acts committed by any one person are considered to be one loss. You can't file a claim for every time the person who stole your card uses it. The whole shopping spree will usually be covered under one claim. This can have a major impact on how stolen cards are insured—since theives tend to use the things

The policy provides up to $500 coverage for lost or stolen credit cards, although federal law limits the liability of the cardholder to $50 per card.

> Similar coverage is also provided for bank cards used at automatic teller machines. However, these cards—especially the so-called "debit cards" which act like credit cards—are sometimes harder to freeze when they've been stolen.

If someone steals your checks and forges your signature, you will be covered under this provision too.

The final coverage available under a typical homeowners policy's additional coverages applies to a **landlord's furnishings**. This coverage was added in 1991 to provide up to $2,500 of coverage (for appliances, household furniture, carpeting, etc.).

We will go into greater detail on what possessions are covered if you are a landlord in Chapter 3.

IF YOU LIVE IN A MOBILE HOME

The owner/occupant of a mobile home faces most of the same property and liability exposures that the owner of a traditional home does. A homeowners policy, when endorsed to cover a mobile home, will usually meet the general coverage needs of the mobile home owner. We will go into greater detail on finding coverage for your personal possessions under a mobile home policy in Chapter 8.

bile home owner. We will go into greater detail on finding coverage for your personal possessions under a mobile home policy in Chapter 8.

CONCLUSION

Homeowners insurance is a good place to start when you are looking to insure your personal possessions. But, if you can't find coverage there, or the limits aren't high enough to insure your valuables, you may want to look elsewhere.

The rest of this book will look into some of the other ways to find coverage for your personal property. Chapter 3 will discuss the benefits of the valuable and affordable renters policy.

3

RENTERS INSURANCE WORKS IN A FEW CASES

On February 18, 1994, Cynthia Silva came home to find that her roommate, Sheryl Stevoff, was entertaining a few friends. At least four of them were smoking cigarettes. At midnight Cynthia went to bed and all but one of the guests went home.

Sheryl and the remaining guest, talked and smoked until 2 a.m. when they went to bed. At 5 a.m. a fire started in the apartment and 20 to 25 of the apartment units in the building sustained damage.

The landlord, who made it a practice to have parents co-sign the lease for student tenants with no income, had paid fire insurance premiums out of the girls' rent. And following the fire, Greater New York Mutual Insurance Company ("GNY"), the insurer of the building, paid out $201,271.93 in damages.

GNY then sought recovery for the damages and alleged that an indemnification clause claimed the tenants were responsible for damages.

The issue was whether the girls and their fathers were co-insured with the landlord or whether they had an independent liability. Clauses in the lease blurred the issue of **tenant liability** for fire damage. They implied that the tenants were only responsible for insuring personal property (through renters insurance).

The lease also suggested that the lessor was responsible for losses not "in" the lessee's premises, that is, everything except the personal property of the lessee. In examining the lease as a whole, the Court held that the lease terms did not provide for liability of the lessee to the lessor for fire damage. The girls were off the hook.

Although Cynthia and Sheryl were not found liable for the damage to the building, the **indemnification clause** in the lease relieved GNY from coverage for the loss of the girls' personal possessions.

Less than half of all renters in the United States bother to insure their personal belongings and furnishings with insurance. People under age 40 are particularly remiss. According to the Western Insurance Information Service (WIIS), renters generally tend to believe that insurance is too expensive, or that they don't own anything valuable enough to insure. Others simply assume that they are covered under the policy owned by their landlord, while others simply aren't aware that renters insurance exists.

Tenant advocacy groups—like Illinois-based Condominium Insurance Specialists of America—estimate that as few as one in four renters in their twenties and thirties buy insurance: Even though the insurance is relatively cheap and easy to get.

Renters insurance is "cheaper than homeowners insurance because you're insuring only your possessions—not the building structure," said Gene Jeffers, executive director of WIIS.

The cost of a typical renter's policy can range from as little as $65 per year up to around $225 a year, depending on the level of coverage and your place of residence.

Millions of people fall victim to the financial hardship of disaster every year. And without renters insurance, you have no protection for your possessions if a theft or fire were to occur. Also you would not be covered for a lawsuit if someone is injured by your possessions.

DO I HAVE ANYTHING WORTH INSURING?

Renters insurance can cover the most expensive to the least expensive of your possessions...including your television, stereo, camera, clothes, furniture, jewelry—even your pots and pans. How much coverage you need depends on the value of your belongings.

If you own just a few hundred dollars of any specific kind of personal property, you probably don't need renters insurance. But, if you care enough about a hobby, sport or other activity to invest thousands of dollars in related equipment, you probably do want to insure those things.

Your possessions can be **tough to value** accurately. An easy way to calculate your insurance needs for a renters policy is to make a list of everything you own that could generally be described as valuable to you. (You may want to refer to the Household Property Inventory Chart in Chapter 1 as a guide.)

Once you've calculated the value of the things you own, you simply have to ask yourself how much of this total you could stand to lose.

ANALUZING YOUR EXPOSURES AS A RENTER

If you are a renter and don't have renters insurance you are setting yourself up for a big loss. Renters are exposed to three major areas of loss:

- additions and alterations;
- personal property; and
- legal liability.

Although it doesn't cover the building itself, renters insurance does provide a limited amount of coverage for **building additions and alterations.** (This coverage is also known as **leasehold improvement insurance**.)This means that if you spend money to improve the apartment or house you're renting—and haven't been reimbursed by your landlord—the renters insurance will cover the investments you've made.

As a renter, however, your most significant property exposure is probably the **personal property** that you own. This includes items such as, stereos, furniture, bedding, clothing, TVs, VCRs, etc. These items are sometimes referred to as **contents**.

As a renter, you are also exposed to **legal liabilities**. If a guest should trip on one of your floor boards, or bump his head on a low ceiling, he could seek damages on the basis of **negligence liability**. As an apartment renter you may also be responsible for injury to other tenants and damage to their belongings. You can also be held liable for injuries or damages which occur off-premises.

For example, you're playing miniature golf with a friend and accidentally swing too high, hitting your friend in the mouth. He may seek damages for the $1,200 dental work he needs as a result of the incident, which would be covered under a renters insurance policy.

The homeowners **HO-4** insurance policy form—called the **renters policy**—is available from most property and casualty insurance companies.

Some confusion comes from the fact that the coverage is called different things by different companies—the **contents broad form**, **broad theft coverage** or **tenants insurance**—but, whatever it's called, the coverage is inexpensive enough to be worth it for just about any renter.

> After experiencing huge industry losses after the Northridge earthquake in California and Florida's Hurricane Andrew, insurance companies are sometimes reluctant to sell policies to renters who live in earthquake or hurricane prone areas.

If you live in an area prone to **natural disasters**, you may consider purchasing supplementary coverage to protect your possessions from damage.

> The more additional coverage that you purchase, the less you will have to pay out of your pocket if a loss occurs.

THE MECHANICS OF RENTERS INSURANCE

All personal property is insured against loss by the **broad form perils** under an HO-4 policy. A homeowners form HO-4 may be issued to any of the following:

- a tenant non-owner of a dwelling or apartment;

- a tenant non-owner of a mobile home;

- an owner-occupant of a condominium unit; or

- an owner-occupant of a dwelling or apartment when not eligible for coverage under one of the combined building and contents homeowner forms.

Renters insurance is purchased most often by renters of apartments, dwellings or condominiums who do not require the complete range of coverages—such as dwelling structure coverage—provided by the other standard homeowners forms. Renters who don't want to pay for liability protection can opt for a policy that covers only personal property.

> If you rent an apartment, you won't need to insure the building structure in which you live.

THE IMPORTANCE OF COVERAGE

When it comes to insuring personal possessions, you—the renter—are on your own. Your landlord's insurance policy offers no protection for your personal property.

Landlords sometimes require that tenants carry some form of renters insurance. (This usually applies to luxury apartments or, conversely, rent-controlled units.)

In states with large urban centers, though, insurance and housing regulators have outlawed these requirements.

However, one should not infer from this legal trend that renters insurance is not worth having. In most markets, it is a **relatively inexpensive** form of insurance coverage.

Renters insurance can either be written in a comprehensive form for **all risks** that aren't explicitly excluded or for **named perils** only. Named perils coverage is about 20 percent less expensive, because the losses covered are usually more limited.

Even insurance written on a named perils basis should cover fire, theft and water damage, because these are the hazards that most renters face.

INSURING AGAINST THEFT

One reason that renters insurance is so attractive is that it covers personal property against theft. **Theft coverage** provides insurance against loss by:

- theft, including attempted theft; and
- vandalism and malicious mischief as a result of theft or attempted theft.

A caveat: The vandalism coverage won't apply if your residence has been vacant for more than 30 consecutive days immediately before the loss.

By comparison, basic dwelling policies do not provide any theft coverage for personal property. A **broad theft coverage endorsement** has to be added to a dwelling policy—at an additional premium—to provide such coverage.

For many insurance companies, the broad theft coverage endorsement—sold in a slightly different version as stand-alone insurance—is renters insurance.

Broad theft policies (or endorsements) contain three definitions that affect the coverage:

- **business** refers to trade, profession or occupation;
- **insured person** means the named insured and residents of the named

insured's household who are either rela-
tives of the named insured or under the
age of 21 and in the care of the insured
person;

- **residence employee** means an employee of the insured who performs duties related to maintenance or use of the
residence, including household or domestic services, or similar duties which are
not related to the business of the insured
person.

It is important to be aware of these definitions when
purchasing a policy. Erroneously read **exclusions**
could cost you a lot of money.

The 1996 Louisiana State Appeals Court decision
Steven G. Crigler vs. David Crigler, et al., shows
the importance of reading the definition of an "insured".

Sherry Johnston and David Crigler lived together for
about thirteen years before co-leasing a house together.
Prior to moving to this house, Sherry acquired a renters policy issued by Allstate which was updated when
they moved. Sherry was the sole insured of this policy.

David's brother, Steven, visited Sherry and David in
July of 1993. One night, the two brothers embarked
on an evening of drinking and stumbled home at 2:00
a.m. They watched TV and continued to drink before David decided to cook french fries for a late
night snack.

He put grease in the pan, turned on the stove, and
went back to the living room where he fell asleep.

Moments later, he awoke to the sounds of fire. As he attempted to douse the flames with water; he splattered hot grease on the floor.

Steven, who had also fallen asleep, woke and ran barefoot into the kitchen, where he slipped and fell into the grease—sustaining severe burns to his feet, ankles, arms and back. Sherry was awakened by the sounds of David putting out the fire. At this point, Steven had already sustained his injuries.

Steven brought suit against his brother, Sherry, and their insurer, Allstate. Allstate denied liability on the part of Ms. Johnston and denied that the policy covered David Crigler.

David and his brother argued that Sherry had known that they had been drinking, that David liked to prepare late night snacks, and that he enjoyed fried foods. So, they argued that it was her duty to warn Steven of the reasonably foreseeable hazards posed by David's behavior.

The court ruled that the brothers were fully aware of David's alcohol consumption, especially since they purchased a six-pack of beer on the way home. The court also ruled that both brothers were awake when David began his ill-fated cooking attempt. Moreover, as a trained chef, David was familiar with the stove, the hazards posed by grease fires, and the proper method to extinguish such a blaze.

Based on these facts, the court ruled that Ms. Johnston owed no duty to warn Steven Crigler about potential hazards related to his brother's behavior.

The Crigler brothers also claimed the policy was ambiguous because it failed to define, the term "spouse"
and that it should include non-marital relationships.
The brothers also alleged that Allstate had accepted
payments from a joint checking account with David's
and Sherry's names and that the Allstate agent knew
the couple lived together out of wedlock.

Allstate argued that Sherry was the only "named insured" of the policy. Sherry Johnston and David
Crigler were not married and David was, therefore,
not Sherry's spouse, nor her relative or a dependent
under her care. Under these terms, the judge concluded that David was not an insured.

The court ruled, that "while modern society tolerates
many forms of inter-personal relationships, we do not
feel that acceptance is wide enough to warrant the
judicial expansion of the term "spouse" to include
one's paramour or concubine, regardless of the merits
or stability of the relationship".

**The term "spouse" implies the existence of a le-
gally recognized marriage and does not lend itself to use as reference to partners living out of
wedlock.**

The term "spouse," as used in the policy, was not suf-
ficiently broad enough to include David. Furthermore,
the common meaning for the term "spouse" is suffi-
ciently uniform to preclude confusion and is not susceptible to multiple interpretations.

THINGS A RENTERS POLICY DOESN'T COVER

Be aware of the following three points, which may affect your coverage:

- Property used for **business purposes** isn't considered personal property and, therefore, isn't covered.

- Only property that belongs to **an insured person** is covered—so, if the $2,000 camera you're keeping for a friend is stolen from your home, you may be liable.

- Property of **residence employees** is covered only if you ask the insurance company to add language saying so. This may raise your premium—though many companies will add the coverage for no additional cost.

LIABILITY LIMITS

A **limit of liability** exists for on-premises coverage. This limit is the most the insurer will pay for any one covered loss at the described location. On-premises coverage applies while the property is:

- at the described location occupied by an insured person;

- in other parts of the described location not occupied exclusively by an insured person (if the property is owned or used by an insured person or covered residence employee); or

- placed for safekeeping in any bank, trust or safe deposit company, public warehouse or occupied dwelling not owned, rented to or occupied by an insured person.

This type of insurance limits coverage either with one general dollar limit or a range of **dollar limits** according to the type of personal property.

In the first case, a policy would insure all your property—regardless of type—to a limit of $20,000. In the second, a policy would insure computer equipment up to $5,000, stereo equipment to $2,000, sports equipment to $1,500, etc.

Although limits of liability are shown for the maximum amount of insurance for any one loss, special **sub-limits of liability** usually apply to specific categories of insured property. Each limit is the most the insurer will pay for each loss for all property in that category. Ask your insurer about the sub-limits of liability that apply to your policy.

Special limits of liability are:

- $200 for money, bank notes, bullion, gold and silver (other than goldware and silverware, platinum, coins and medals);

- $1,000 for securities, accounts, deeds, evidences of debt, letters of credit, notes (other than bank notes), manuscripts, passports, tickets and stamps;

- $1,000 for watercraft (including their trailers), furnishings, equipment and outboard motors;

- $1,000 for trailers not used with water-craft;

- $1,000 for jewelry, watches, furs, precious and semiprecious stones;

- $2,000 for firearms;

- $2,500 for silverware, silver-plated ware, goldware, gold-plated ware, and pewterware, including flatware, hollowware, tea sets, trays and trophies.

> If you purchased a new computer for $10,000 and your policy has a $6,000 limit, you may want to shop for a new policy or buy a floater to cover the computer's full value.

Homeowners policies have similar limits. The policy is intended to provide **basic coverage** for special items of value which may be subject to theft. Most policies will not allow the full limit of liability to be applied to a specific kind of property.

OFF-PREMISES THEFT COVERAGE

In some cases, **off-premises theft coverage** is available. Off-premises coverage applies while the property is away from the described location if the property is either:

- owned or used by an insured person; or

- owned by a residence employee while in an insured dwelling, or while engaged in the employ of an insured.

Example: If you ride your $2,000 mountain bike from the houseboat you're renting to the mountains north of Seattle and someone steals it while you're waiting to pay for a cafe latte, the insurance company will pay for a new bike.

The following conditions apply to off-premises coverage:

- it can only be bought if you also have **on-premises coverage**;

- a separate limit of liability must be shown for off-premises coverage (this limit— usually lower than on-premises limits— is the most the insurer will pay for any one loss);

- off-premises coverage does not apply to property that you move to a newly acquired principal residence.

This last point is often an issue in renters insurance.

Insurance companies often limit the **transferability** of a renters policy from one location to another.

If you move during the policy term to a new **principal residence**, the limit of liability for **on-premises coverage** will apply at each residence and in transit between them for a period of 30 days after you begin to move the property.

When the moving is completed, on-premises coverage applies at the new described location only.

THINGS BROAD THEFT DOESN'T COVER

Broad theft coverage does not apply to the following types of property:

- aircraft and parts, other than model or hobby aircraft;

- animals, birds or fish;

- business property of an insured person or residence employee on or away from the described location;

- credit cards and fund transfer cards;

- motor vehicles, other than motorized equipment which is not subject to motor vehicle registration and which is used to service the described location, or is designed to assist the handicapped;

- motor vehicle equipment and any device for the transmitting, recording, receiving or reproduction of sound or pictures which is operated by power from the electrical system of a motorized vehicle, including tapes, wires, discs or other media for use with such device, while in or upon the vehicle;

- property held as a sample or for sale or delivery after sale;

- property of tenants, roomers and boarders not related to an insured person;

- property separately described and specifically insured by any other insurance;

- property while at any other location owned, rented to or occupied by any insured person, except while an insured person is temporarily residing there;

- property while in the custody of any laundry, cleaner, tailor, presser or dyer except for loss by burglary or robbery;

- property while in the mail.

You may recognize some of these exclusions from standard homeowners and dwelling policies.

The broad theft form adds **two conditions** that can influence whether or not personal property (which would otherwise be covered) is covered:

- Theft coverage requires the insured person to notify the police of a theft.

- If theft is also covered by another type of insurance, the insurance company is only obligated to pay the proportion of the loss that the limit of liability under the theft endorsement bears to the total amount of insurance.

WHEN YOU'RE THE LANDLORD

Of course, tenants aren't the only ones who may need property insurance in a rental situation. If you're renting out an apartment or house that you own, you have significant exposures to financial loss.

Fortunately, you can protect yourself against some rental losses. With some modifications, a combina-

tion of dwelling insurance and broad theft coverage
should meet your needs.

> If your tenant should steal something, the chances
> are good that you won't collect on a basic dwell-
> ing policy—which only insures the house and
> contents against loss and damage from fire, wind,
> smoke, vandalism and other hazards. That is why
> it is important to have the same theft coverage
> that the renters themselves should be buying.

If a theft occurs, and your insurance finds you negligent (for example, if you have forgotten to double
latch the door or secure a window), it might resist
paying for some stolen items. Low premium rates
for its standard coverage are based on the assump-
tion that you will be responsible for **keeping the
home and contents safe**. The company might pay
for such things as a stolen television set and furniture—but not for missing jewelry, furs, silver, coins
and watches.

Before you accept a renter's deposit check. Reread your
homeowners or dwelling policy. If the exclusions or
conditions section has a policy that reads:

> "...peril of theft does not include any part of
> loss when the property is rented by the in-
> sured to another party."

You may want to convert to an **all-risk** homeowners
policy or buy an **endorsement** broadening your theft
coverage. As noted earlier, you can expect to pay
as much as 20 percent more than the cost of a basic
policy for all-risk coverage. The endorsement to theft
coverage will usually cost less than this—but still

more than a standard theft package.

If you rent your home frequently, or own more than one property which you rent out, you may need a **multi-peril policy**. This kind of insurance—which is actually a commercial policy—is designed for professional landlords. It covers just about every exposure a landlord faces and can be modified to insure against various risks. But, if you're just renting one house or apartment, you'll probably do best to use **endorsements** to a standard homeowners or dwelling policy.

Some part-time landlords may be tempted to avoid the extra insurance by simply failing to mention to the insurance company that a theft occurred while the property was rented. But this is not advisable.

CONCLUSION

Choosing not to buy insurance can be a big mistake. Even if you are not a homeowner you probably have belongings of value (at least to you). Fortunately for consumers, there are policies available for renters to insure protection in case of theft and more. And renters insurance is one kind of coverage that most people agree is a bargain.

In the next chapter, we will discuss how to find coverage for your possessions under a personal auto policy.

4

AUTO INSURANCE COVERS JUST A LITTLE

Insurance is a necessity if you drive a car, but if you are looking for coverage that extends to your personal possessions, you may have to look close and read the fine print.

The **personal auto policy** is designed to provide a broad package of coverage that generally satisfies only the automobile insurance needs of most individuals and families. However, if you look over your policy you will find coverage for a small number of your personal possessions, as well.

Auto insurance is designed to reduce many of the financial losses that could otherwise result from owning or operating a car, including the loss of your personal possessions. This is why it is important that you understand the fundamentals of how auto coverage applies to your personal possessions.

WHY YOU BUY AUTO INSURANCE

Usually, the main reason you buy auto insurance is

that the law says you have to have it. This mandated insurance covers your liability exposure for any damage that you may cause to other people or their property. Most states call these laws your **financial responsibility requirements.**

In most cases, coverage under an automobile insurance policy applies to a variety of exposures arising out of the ownership, maintenance or use of automobiles.

Auto insurance has two significant elements: **liability coverage** for damage you do to other people or property; **collision (or comprehensive) coverage** for damage you do to yourself or your own property.

PERSONAL PROPERTY

Most **contents** of a vehicle, are not covered under a standard auto policy. This may seem unfair, because all drivers carry belongings around in their cars.

But, in order to make the risk projections for auto insurance feasible, insurance companies can not calculate losses of personal possessions because they vary so much.

When you buy insurance for your car, the premiums that the insurance company charges for **physical damage coverage** ("collision" and "other than collision") are based on the maximum amount that the insurance company might have to pay if the vehicle were a total loss.

But, this does not include the personal property in your car at the time of loss.

> For example, the insurance company might charge $200 for one year's coverage on an $8,000 car. The most the company could expect to pay to repair or replace the car would be $8000. It has no control over the value of any items you might carry in the vehicle on any given day. If you were transporting a $100,000 painting in an $8,000 car and the car and painting were destroyed in a collision, the insurance company would be unfairly penalized if it had to pay out $108,000 when it had collected a premium for only $8,000.

Personal property items (such as clothing, cameras, sporting equipment, tools and all the things that you carry around in your car) should be insured under a different type of policy.

Most people have coverage for these items under a **homeowners policy**, but coverage is also available under **personal property floaters** and other types of specialized property insurance forms.

> If you haven't insured those expensive golf clubs your wife bought you last year for your birthday, don't leave them on the back seat of your car over an extended period of time, because you won't find coverage for them under your auto policy in the case of a theft.

Your auto insurance policy also does not provide coverage for damage to any property of others in your possession. If, for example, you backed over a lawn mower that you borrowed from a neighbor, there would be no coverage. This exclusion does not apply (therefore, coverage is granted) for property damage to residences or garages that you don't own.

A FEW THINGS THAT ARE COVERED

Though an auto policy does not cover most personal possessions, it will cover the following:

- Sound reproduction equipment and accessories are covered only if permanently installed in the vehicle. (If the equipment was permanently installed where the car manufacturers would normally not install it, it would not be covered.

- An appreciable number of late model cars have computers which monitor engine performance or make diagnoses. A few have electronic map guides. This equipment is covered if necessary to the operation of the vehicle. Other equipment may also be covered if it is part of the same unit housing the sound equipment, and if it is permanently installed.

COMMON EXCLUSIONS

Exclusions involve some of the most heated—and most often litigated—disputes over insurance language. Some exclusions exist simply to remove coverage for **above-average risk factors** which are not anticipated in average rates and premiums. The coverage is available for an additional charge.

This is the case with **audio, visual and data equipment** and the tapes, records and other media used with this equipment, because they have an above average exposure to theft.

Typically, a personal auto policy excludes coverage for:

electronic equipment designed for sound reproduction, including radios and stereos, tape decks or compact disc players; and any other electronic equipment that receives or transmits audio, visual or data signals, including, citizens band radios, telephones, two-way mobile radios, scanning monitor receivers, television monitor receivers, video cassette recorders, audio cassette recorders, or personal computers, tapes, records, disc or other media used with the above equipment. (This exclusion does not apply if the equipment is permanently installed in the dashboard or console of your car.)

The physical damage section of the personal auto policy excludes many items which are easily removed or damaged, or are considered to be "extra" accessories, but a number of endorsements allow you to "buy back" these exclusions.

To keep up with advances in modern technology, the exclusion now applies to such devices as car telephones, television monitors, video cassette recorders and personal computers.

> Don't leave your laptop computer in your car if you don't have coverage for it under another policy.

If you have a radar detector in your car when a loss occurs, your policy will probably exclude coverage for the replacement of the detector.

Radar detectors are used to determine where the police have set up radar to enforce the speed limit. Because the purpose of radar detectors is to help drivers avoid obeying speed laws, and because such equipment is outlawed in some states, insurance companies are usually unwilling to provide coverages for these devices under an auto policy.

If you purchase a camper body or a trailer and it's not listed in the Declarations section of your policy, it is excluded from coverage. However, this does not apply if you have acquired a new camper body or trailer during the policy period, if your insurer has been notified within 30 days.

COVERAGE FOR TAPES, RECORDS OR OTHER DEVICES

In the standard personal auto policy, a number of exclusions remove coverage for tapes, records and other media and accessories used with audio, visual and data equipment. If you keep a number of tapes or compact discs in your car, you might choose to purchase coverage for these items by endorsement.

> Coverage for this sort of personal property is usu-
> ally sold with low liability limits—usually less than
> $500 often less than $250.

This endorsement will be attached to the policy or a **change of endorsement** when issued after the policy is written, and an additional premium will be charged.

The endorsement for tapes and records provides limited coverage for media used with sound equipment and other equipment—but it does not cover the equipment itself. For example, it would not cover the loss of a two-way radio, car phone or other device.

More complete coverage can be obtained by purchasing **Coverage for Audio, Visual and Data Electronic Equipment and Tapes, Records, Discs and Other Media endorsement**. This endorsement covers equipment (such as two-way radios, FAX machines, car phones), as well as the media used with the equipment.

> In order for coverage to apply, the equipment
> must either be permanently installed in the auto
> or removable from a housing unit which is per-
> manently installed in your covered auto or any
> nonowned auto. It must be designed to be oper-
> ated solely by the auto's electrical power system.
> The equipment must receive, transmit or record
> audio, visual or data signals.

No coverage is provided under this endorsement for devices used solely to reproduce sound or that monitor the car's operating system (such devices are covered under the standard coverage—as long as they are permanently installed).

Coverage for audio, visual and data electronic equipment is written for a specified dollar amount, while coverage for tapes, discs and other media is still subject to a lower limit. Losses are paid at the lowest of three values: the limit of insurance, the actual cash value, or the amount necessary to repair or replace the property.

CUSTOM AND AFTER MARKET EQUIPMENT

A standard auto policy excludes coverage for loss to awnings, cabanas, or equipment designed to create additional living facilities that are part of a camper or van. However, if you need coverage for this kind of property, an endorsement can be added for an additional premium.

> Coverage for loss to custom furnishings or equipment may be added under **customizing equipment coverage endorsement** for an additional premium.

If you drive a recreational vehicle or a so-called "custom van conversion," you probably have **custom furnishings and equipment**, such as camper kitchen equipment, carpeting, sleeping facilities, etc. An endorsement for your auto policy covers the following **customized equipment** in a pick-up or van:

- special carpeting and insulation, furniture, bars or television receivers;

- facilities for cooking and sleeping;

- height-extending roofs; and

- custom murals, paintings or other decals or graphics.

INSURING YOUR STUFF WHEN IT'S IN A RENTAL CAR

A frequently asked question about car insurance is: Do I need to buy insurance when I rent a car?

When you rent a car, one of the employees at the rental company usually will shove a piece of paper in your face while asking whether you would like insurance coverage. The piece of paper, a **collision damage waiver** (CDW), is designed to release you from any responsibility for damage to the rental car (provided you comply with the rental contract terms). If you decline the coverage and have an accident, you may be responsible for the entire value of the rental car.

A CDW, highly overpriced (adding as much as $11 a day to the cost of renting a car), has limitations for such things as driving on an unpaved road, or engaging in negligent driving (the car-rental company's definition of negligent). If a car renter violates these restrictions, he or she won't be covered.

Besides the CDW, a rental-car company may try to sell you **personal-effects coverage**. This coverage provides you with limited reimbursement for loss of baggage and other personal property during the rental period.

> When you rent a car, the rental agent may try to sell you up to four different kinds of supplemental insurance: Collision damage waiver (CDW), personal accident, extra liability, and personal effects. The coverage often duplicates insurance that you already carry.

Generally, your own auto insurance will cover collision damage to the car you rent and most likely for liability in case you hurt someone or damage someone else's property. And your homeowners policy may cover your personal effects, even when you're on a trip. So, be sure to check out the limits on your homeowners policy—they tend to vary, especially with high-value personal possessions such as computers and jewelry.

> If you experience a loss out of a vehicle such as a motor home, trailer or camper located as a residence, it's not covered under your auto policy. However, If you use your car as a regular residence, then items from your car might be covered under your homeowners or mobile home policy.

LIMIT OF LIABILITY

Under your auto policy your insurance company is liable for the actual cash value or the cost to repair or replace the damaged or stolen property, whichever is less. However, coverage for a non-owned trailer is limited to $500. In all settlements, depreciation and the condition of the vehicle are considered in determining the ACV at the time of loss.

Stolen property may be returned to the insured person, and payment made for any damage, or the company may keep the property and pay the insured an agreed or appraised amount in money.

CONCLUSION

As you can see, there are more situations than you would assume in which your auto policy provides coverage for your possessions. But, if you need coverage tailored to a specific item, you may want to check out the next chapter on personal property floaters. This type of coverage *floats* with the property wherever it goes—even in the car.

AUTO INSURANCE COVERS JUST A LITTLE

HOW PROPERTY
FLOATERS WORK

If a bad storm or an accident at sea caused you to lose your prized thoroughbred horse, coverage would be provided under a **marine insurance policy**.

Originally, marine insurance referred exclusively to seagoing risks. (This refers back to the origins of Lloyd's of London mentioned in Chapter 1.) A bad storm, an accident at sea, a careless docking and a loss to hull, cargo, and even life could be immense. Such risks still exist, and are the province of **ocean marine insurance**.

Cargo coming under the realm of ocean marine must be transported beyond its ocean terminal. Usually done by truck or railroad— the continuation of the journey of ocean cargo over land is covered under **inland marine** insurance.

> Today, even the transportation of goods over land, whether or not they have moved over water, is the subject of inland marine insurance.

It was a short step from the concept of marine in-surance to the concept of inland marine covering any movable property (as distinct from property in-surance on say, a house or a place of business).

For this reason, the special insurance written on these items is still referred to as inland marine, even if the item is as remote from oceangoing vessels as an expensive jewelry collection, a racehorse, or even your camera equipment. Such policies are **inland marine coverages**, and sometimes are called **floaters**, due to the fact that the insurance is written on items that *float* or move about.

> **A floater is a form of insurance that applies to movable property, whatever its location, if it is within the territorial limits imposed by the con-tract. The coverage "floats" with the property.**

PROPERTY FLOATERS

If you own valuable personal property which is of-ten moved around, you may need a broader and more comprehensive coverage than the coverage provided by your homeowners or dwelling policy.

Floaters provide an **extended coverage** with re-spect to the perils that are covered. They are gener-ally written to cover direct physical loss to a de-scribed property except for certain exclusions.

A typical homeowners policy limits coverage for spe-cific kinds of property. However, it's important to know what these limits are. A standard policy will usually provide coverage up to the following limits:

1. $200 on **money**, **bank notes**, bullion, **gold** other than goldware, silverware, platinum, **coins** and **medals**;

2. $1,000 on **securities**, deeds, evidences of debt, **letters of credit**, notes other than bank notes, manuscripts, **personal records**, passports, tickets and **stamps**;

3. $1,000 on **watercraft**, including their trailers, furnishings, equipment and outboard engines or motors;

4. $1,000 on **trailers** not used with watercraft;

5. $1,000 for loss by theft of **jewelry, watches, furs**, precious and semi-precious stones;

6. $2,000 for loss by theft of **firearms**;

7. $2500 for loss by theft of **silverware**, silver-plated ware, goldware, gold-plated ware and pewterware (this includes flatware, holloware, tea sets, trays and trophies made of or including gold, silver or pewter);

8. $2500 on property on the "residence premises," used any time or in any manner for **any "business" purpose**;

9. $250 on property away from the "residence premises," used at any time or in any manner for any "business" purpose;

10. $1000 on **grave markers**.

> These limits may change over time—but they tend
> to stay constant in relation to one another and as
> a percentage of the overall policy limits.

Notice that items 5, 6 and 7 are **theft-only limita-tions**. The other limitations apply to all perils. (As ever, broader coverage is available for several of these items through floaters.)

A standard homeowners policy also will pay up to $1,000 for loss to **electronic apparatus**—accessories, antennas, tapes, wires, records, discs or other media—while in a motor vehicle, if the electronic apparatus is "equipped to be operated by power from the electrical system of the vehicle or conveyance while retaining its capability of being operated by other sources of power."

On a related note, a standard policy also will cover up to $1,000 for loss to electronic apparatus, while not in a motor vehicle, if the electronic apparatus is "operated by power from the vehicle's electrical system or conveyance while retaining its capability of being operated by other sources of power, is away from the *residence premises*, and is used at any time or in any manner for any business purpose."

> These dense paragraphs mean the policy will
> cover cell phones, eletronics and office-type ap-
> pliances that can be charged up in your home,
> office or car.

Depending upon the form used, coverage may be written on a **scheduled** (per item) basis or a **blanket** (per class) basis.

WHERE A FLOATER FITS IN

A **personal property floater** (PPF), covers personal property owned or used by you that is normally kept at your home. The PPF also offers worldwide coverage on the same property when it is temporarily away from your home and it is insured on an **all-risks** basis—meaning that all direct losses will be covered unless they are specifically excluded.

The PPF insures the following property, which is either not covered or covered to a certain limit in a standard homeowners policy:

- silverware, goldware, and pewterware;
- clothing;
- rugs and draperies;
- musical instruments and electronic equipment;
- paintings and other art objects;
- china and glassware;
- cameras and photographic equipment;
- guns and sports equipment;
- major appliances;
- bedding and linens;
- furniture;
- all other personal property, and professional books and equipment while in your home; and
- building additions and alterations.

The amount of insurance available in each class is the maximum limit of recovery for any one loss in that category. Adding these up will give you the **total policy limit**. Check with an insurer specifically on the total limits available.

UNSCHEDULED PROPERTY

Unscheduled personal property typically requires a $100 deductible for each separate loss, but, if you want to reduce your premium, a higher deductible is also available.

A standard homeowners policy will cover unscheduled personal property on a named perils basis. But, you may own some valuable personal property which would be better covered if it were scheduled and specifically insured under a floater policy. **High-value** property—such as jewelry, fur coats, etc.—generally falls into this category.

If you own any of the following items, you may want to consider purchasing a floater policy:

- **unique objects**, including works of art, antiques, paintings and collections of unusual property (such as a valuable stamp or coin collection);
- **portable property**, including cameras and camera equipment, musical instruments or sports equipment;
- **fragile articles**, with a high value such as glassware, scientific instruments or computers;

- **business or professional equipment**, which a homeowners policy only insures for $2,500 at your home and $250 away from your home, can be insured more adequately by scheduling the property with a stated amount of insurance.

Be sure to establish the value of all property in advance—by doing this, you will avoid having to prove its value after a loss occurs.

EXCLUSIONS

The following types of property are **not covered** under a personal property floater:

- **animals**, fish and birds;

- **boats, aircraft**, trailers and campers;

- **motor vehicles** designed for transportation or recreational use;

- equipment and furnishings for the above vehicles unless removed from the vehicle and located at your place of residence;

- owned **property of a business**, profession or occupation (except books, instruments and equipment, which is covered while in your home); and

- property usually kept somewhere other than your place of residence throughout the year.

In addition to the property not covered under a personal property floater, a floater also has specific losses which are excluded from coverage. These include **losses caused by**:

- **animals** owned or kept by you;

- insects or vermin;

- marring or scratching of property, breakage of glass or other fragile articles (except if caused by fire, lightning, theft, vandalism or malicious mischief and certain other perils);

- mechanical or structural **breakdown** (except by fire);

- **wear and tear**, deterioration or what policies call "**inherent vice**";

- **dampness** or extreme changes of temperature (except if caused by rain, snow, sleet, hailing or bursting of pipes or other apparatus);

- any work on covered property (other than jewelry, watches and furs);

- acts or decisions of any person, organization or **governmental body**; and

- water damage.

If you're planning to get **divorced**, you may want to obtain your own floater policy because, chances are, you won't find coverage at the expense of your ex's insurer. Take for example, the case of *Georgia Ball v. the Aetna Casualty and Surety Company and the Standard Fire Insurance Company,* in which a plaintiff sought recovery from her former husband's policy.

Aetna Casualty & Surety Company issued a property floater policy to Glenn Ball which covered personal property owned, used or worn by Ball and his family residing in the same household. The policy's schedule contained a **typewritten list** of items and their values. Several of these items were missing from the address indicated on the policy.

During this period, Georgia and Glenn had been experiencing marital difficulties. On the date that the items disappeared, Glenn was staying in a hotel.

Georgia requested coverage for the missing items and Aetna refused to honor her demands because she wasn't part of Glenn's household by reason of their marital problems, separation and eventual divorce. Also, the insurance company said the values noted on the policy's schedule didn't reflect the true worth of the missing items.

The court eventually ruled:

> 1. Factual matters, such as attempted reconciliation, pendency of a divorce action, frequency and duration of absences from home, and financial responsibility are significant as they reflect the parties' claimed intent.

> 2. [Georgia] claimed that the valuations found on the schedule of the so-called "valued policy" were binding upon Aetna. However, Aetna claimed that...its liability, if any, was limited to the actual cash value of the missing items.

> 3. The appraisal and incorporation of a schedule does not necessarily indicate a

valued policy, since there are a number of other reasons why the insurer would want such information.

4. While it is preferable that the identification of contractual obligations be confined to the document itself, any ambiguity requires an analysis of the surrounding circumstances as they reflect the parties' intent— a question of fact which should not be settled by summary judgment.

The court overruled Mrs. Ball's request for summary judgment on the manner and **Aetna was not required to pay**.

PERSONAL EFFECTS FLOATER

If you are planning on taking a trip, you may want to consider a **personal effects floater** (PEF), designed for people who want to cover their personal possessions while traveling.

> A PEF provides "all-risk" coverage for your property anywhere in the world— but only while the covered property is away from the residence premises and only for you, your spouse, and any unmarried children who live with you.

Personal effects refers to any personal property that you would normally wear or carry. It is designed to cover items such as **luggage, clothes, cameras**, and **sports equipment**, while you are traveling or on vacation.

A PEF excludes coverage for:

- automobiles, motorcycles, bicycles, boats and other conveyances and their accessories;

- accounts, bills, currency, deeds, evidence of debt and letters or credit;

- passports, documents, money, securities and transportation or other tickets;

- household furniture and animals;

- automobile equipment, business samples, and medical equipment;

- contact lenses and artificial teeth or limbs; and

- merchandise for sale or exhibition, theatrical property and property specifically insured.

> Property covered under a personal effects floater must be used or worn by you and it must also belong to you. If you borrow property from anyone else other than another insured, you will not be covered for its loss.

Under the PEF, your personal effects are covered on an "all-risks" basis except for:

- damage to personal effects from normal wear and tear, gradual deterioration, insects, vermin, inherent vice or damage while they are being repaired;

- breakage of brittle articles unless a result of theft, fire or accident to a conveyance;

- damage to effects while at your place of residence;

- damage to effects while property is in storage. (However, if you store your luggage in a locker at the airport or train station while traveling or vacationing, the exclusion does not apply.);

- any damage to effects while in the custody of a student at school—except for loss by fire.

Other **personal effects** are also subject to limitations of coverage. For example: Coverage for any single piece of jewelry, watches or furs is usually limited to 10 percent of the total amount of insurance with a maximum of $100.

You won't find coverage for theft of personal effects from an unattended automobile under a personal effects floater. However, coverage would apply if the car was locked and there were visible marks of forcible entry. The amount paid would be limited to a maximum of 10 percent of the total amount of insurance or $250, whichever is lower.

INDIVIDUAL ARTICLES FLOATER

In addition to the personal effects floater, a number of **individual articles floaters** can insure specific types of personal property for scheduled amounts.

Usually issued as inland marine forms, separate floaters are available to insure bicycles, cameras, fine
art, **golf equipment**, jewelry and furs, musical instruments, stamp and coin collections, silverware,
and more.

When you are insuring your personal property for
scheduled amounts, be sure to know the exact
value of your property. This may cost you time and
money—but it will save you a bundle of money in a
lawsuit. Take a look at this case, in which parties
argued the correct appraised value of property.

Francis Maxwell, a Dean of Educational Adminis-
tration at Belleville Area College in Illinois and collector of art objects, purchased 14 separate oriental
art objects from Charles Bueche for $19,800.

Bueche also furnished Maxwell with an appraisal
of the 14 pieces of art in which he stated their value
to be $275,800.

A month later, Maxwell made a request for coverage of fine art works through a local broker—but he
failed to advise Lloyd's that the dealer who had appraised the art at a value of $275,800 was the same
dealer who sold him the art for only $19,800. Lloyd's
issued Maxwell a cover note of insurance on the
objects in the amount of the appraisal.

On or about March 6 of the next year, all of the
items, were stolen from Maxwell's apartment and
he notified Lloyd's of his loss.

In an investigation, Lloyd's discovered the great dis-
crepancy between what Maxwell paid for the works
of art and their appraised value. They also learned

that the seller of the art objects had also furnished the appraisals and had declined payment, but offered to refund the premium Maxwell had paid.

Maxwell filed suit and sought to recover $245,800 for the stolen items. At the trial, Lloyd's presented evidence which showed that the art items were **not of the value** and nature Maxwell had represented them to be. Bueche's valuations were also brought into question by investigating his initial acquisition of the pieces of art.

The court ruled that the value of the items did not remotely resemble items of the value of $275,800 and that had the transaction between Maxwell and Bueche been submitted, coverage would not have been issued.

However, the court found that Maxwell was under no duty to report the source and purchase price of the art objects because **Lloyd's did not ask** him to and therefore, did not enter into a planned scheme to defraud Lloyd's. Furthermore, they concluded that only the most naive—or the most blissfully ignorant—person could believe that he could purchase genuine objects of art valued at $275,800 from an established art dealer and appraiser for less than one-thirteenth of their value.

You can purchase an individual floater when you need to insure personal property that is concentrated in one or two classes of property. When there is a need to insure multiple classes of property, it is more practical to use a personal articles floater.

PERSONAL ARTICLES FLOATER

The **personal articles floater** (PAF) is a basic form used to insure certain classes of personal property on an itemized and scheduled basis. It is almost identical to the scheduled personal property endorsement which may be attached to a homeowners policy.

The standard PAF usually contains a **pre-printed schedule** which includes the following classes of insurable property:

- jewelry;
- furs;
- cameras;
- musical instruments;
- silverware;
- golf equipment;
- fine art;
- stamps; and
- coins (coins include paper money and bank notes owned by or in the custody or control of the insured).

For each **class of property** covered, an amount of insurance must be shown and the article(s) must be described.

Other classes of property may be included in the PAF, but they are generally subject to the appropriate rates and forms. Depending upon your insurer, the pre-printed schedule may include **lines** referring to boats and other items.

> You may want to purchase a scheduled personal property floater to provide coverage that is similar to the personal articles floater for valuable items that don't fall within the above categories.

Scheduled personal property floaters can be purchased to cover almost any type of property, including dentures, typewriters, camping equipment, wheelchairs, stereo equipment, grandfather clocks, etc. To obtain this type of coverage, contact your insurance company about which **unfiled forms** which can be adapted to meet your needs.

NEWLY ACQUIRED PROPERTY

If you have **newly acquired property**, check your PAF. You may find that it provides automatic coverage for a limited period of time. For coverage to apply, an amount of insurance must already be scheduled for the property class.

> A caveat: You usually have to report the acquisition of property to your insurance company. If you don't report it, there may be no coverage.

If you acquire any new jewelry, furs, cameras or musical instruments, the personal articles floater will cover you for the actual cash value of your property up to $10,000 or 25 percent of the amount of insurance already scheduled—whichever is less.

When you buy a mink coat, you have 30 days from the date of purchase to report the sartorial indulgence to your insurer in order for coverage to apply.

Your PAF also will only cover you for the **actual cash value** up to 25 percent of the amount of insurance already scheduled for newly acquired **fine art**. However, make sure that you report the item to your insurance company within 90 days.

If fine art is insured, the coverage applies only within the United States and Canada.

WHAT'S COVERED?

The personal articles floater will insure your property against all risks of **direct physical loss** except losses caused by war, wear and tear, deterioration, inherent vice and insects or vermin.

Additional **exclusions** apply to specific classes of property. For example: Damage to immobile musical instruments won't be covered if caused by repairs or adjustments. So watch the piano tuner. However, any damage by fire or explosion is covered.

If your Renoir painting is insured and you display it at an art exhibit at the local fairgrounds, damage will not be covered unless the **exhibition premises** are covered by your policy.

If a loss to a pair or set occurs, a PAF will pay you the full scheduled amount for the set only if you surrender the remaining articles of the set.

All scheduled property other than fine art is covered on an **actual cash value** basis. But the policy won't pay more than the stated amount of insurance—or the amount for which you could be expected to repair or replace the property.

If you suffer a loss to **a pair or a set** for any property other than fine art, your insurance company has the option to repair or replace any part of the pair or set, or pay the difference between the actual cash value of the property before and after loss.

> Breakage of glass objects of art, statuary marble, porcelain, and similar fragile items is covered only when caused by fire, lightning, explosions, windstorm, earthquake, flood, malicious damage, theft or derailment or overturn of a conveyance. All-risk glass coverage may be purchased, too.

Unscheduled **stamps or coins** that are covered on a **blanket basis** (multiple types of property at a single location or one or more types of property at multiple locations) are insured for their market value. However, coverage for any single stamp or coin is limited to $250 and coverage for any one coin collection is limited to $1,000.

> Losses to your stamp or coin collections are not covered if caused by fading, creasing, scratching, tearing, transfer of colors, inherent defect, dampness, extremes of temperature, depreciation, theft from an unattended automobile and damage from being handled or worked on.

Stamps and coins also aren't covered while they are in the custody of transportation companies or during the process of shipment by any form of non-registered mail. And they won't be covered for disappearance unless each item is described in the policy and scheduled with a specific amount of insurance.

> **All stamps or coins covered by a personal articles floater must be part of a collection.**

There are a number of conditions that appear in a floater covering your personal property. The most important include:

- **Loss Settlement.** With a few exceptions, the amount paid for a covered loss is the lowest of the following:

    1. the actual cash value at the time of loss or damage;
    2. the amount for which the insured could reasonably be expected to have property repaired to its condition before the loss;
    3. the amount for which the insured could reasonably be expected to replace the property with property most identical to the item lost or damaged; or
    4. the amount of insurance stated in the policy.

- **Loss to a Pair, Set or Parts**. In the event of property damage or loss to a pair or set (such as loss of one candelabra) the amount paid is not based on a total loss—the insurer may choose to:

    1. repair or replace any part to restore the set to its value before loss; or

2. Pay the difference between the actual cash value of the property before and after the loss.

- **Claim against others**. Similar to the subrogation clause, if a loss occurs and your insurer believes that it can recover the loss payment from the person or parties responsible, a payment of loss to you would be considered a loan. This means that any recovery you would receive from others after you have received your loan would have to be paid to the insurance company.

- **Insurance Not to Benefit Others**. This provision states that no other person or organization that has custody of the property and is paid for services can benefit from the property's insurance. A third party who was responsible for the loss would not be able to deny liability for payment because the property is insured. Thus, the insurance company's right of subrogation against the negligent party is retained.

- **Other Insurance**. If you have any other insurance that applies to the property at a time of loss (not including this policy), the insurance would be considered excess over the other insurance.

OTHER FLOATERS

Some insurers offer a number of floaters to meet special needs. Here are just a few.

Wedding presents floater. This floater is a short term (typically 90 days) policy which covers the wedding presents of the bride and groom while on their honeymoon. Permanent coverage is available under a homeowners or renters policy—but in some situations there is a need for temporary coverage. However, breakage to fragile items is excluded, as well as several classes of property: vehicles, real estate, money, etc.

Trip transit floater. This is the personal property floater version of similar **commercial floaters**, sold by many travel agencies. Designed to cover one's personal property for just one trip (the one made, for instance, from the insured's old residence to a new one), a trip transit form usually covers loss from fire, flood and transportation perils. Coverage for other perils, such as theft, can be purchased by endorsement.

Sports memorabilia. Growing in popularity, this floater is used to insure all sorts of sport-related items (not just trading cards).

You may want to insure those O.J. cards now that you've been showing them off to your neighbors. They may be worth even more in the future than they're worth now.

Most insurers don't have a standard policy to cover these, sometimes extensive, collections. Some **specialty brokers** provide coverage on either a blanket or a scheduled basis—and can cover the items even while in transit or off premises.

> You may even want to check with the sports memorabilia store where you do most of your business. Usually, dealers know of brokers who handle such items.

Large coin and stamp collections. Although the scheduled personal property endorsement or a personal articles floater covers coins and stamps, it may not provide adequate coverage for the special needs of a large collector. In many cases, coverage is limited (mysterious disappearance is not covered), and the property may only get limited coverage while on exhibition. (Coin and stamp collectors often take their collections to exhibitions to trade and sell items.)

> The most customized coverage which the serious collector can obtain is through membership in either the American Philatelic Society (stamps), or the American Numismatic Society (coins). Group coverage is also available through these organizations.

Sports equipment. This is another class which can present significant exposures. Large gun collections and their auxiliary equipment, as well as equipment used in other types of sport (archery, fishing, etc.) can be worth a significant amount of money.

> You may need this coverage because a typical personal articles floater will only cover the guns themselves and none of the related equipment, (nor will it cover sports equipment of any other nature—archery or the like).

High-value fine art. For people who are fond of collecting fine art, the value of an individual item or the total value scheduled for all items may exceed the amount of coverage which standard property insurers are willing or able to provide. A number of excess and surplus lines brokerage houses provide coverage for these larger needs.

A vital consideration when considering a miscellaneous floater is whether or not it provides an agreed-upon amount of coverage. Many of the specialty policies do provide coverage on this basis.

CONCLUSION

Many types of property have special coverage needs. Homeowners policies often do not adequately cover such property because of special (low) limits of liability, and coverage that applies on a named-perils basis.

A variety of floater forms are available to fill some of these insurance gaps. Many classes of personal property may be insured under personal articles floaters or personal property floaters for higher amounts than are available under homeowners policies.

This chapter has given you the essential tools for finding broader coverage than named perils forms. If your insurance company won't cover the type of property discussed in this chapter, or will provide coverage only at very low limits while the property is away from the insured location—a floater may be right for you.

6

HOW UMBRELLA
COVERAGE WORKS

As the number of outrageous tort lawsuits and punitive damages continues to rise throughout the country, the popularity of personal umbrella insurance policies continues to grow.

"The more people read the papers, the more they become concerned about their own exposures," says one New York-based insurance agent.

After you have conducted an inventory of all your personal assets and find that your assets are much greater than the liability limits of your homeowners or renters policy, you may want to purchase an additional "umbrella" policy that will extend your liability coverage to $1 million or more.

As we've seen, the **liability limit** on a policy is the maximum amount which will be paid for any one **occurrence**.(An occurrence is defined as an accident or a continuous or repeated exposure over a period of time which causes a loss or injury.)

Liability judgments can exceed the liability limits of

your policy. After these limits have been exhausted—
you may be forced to pay with your personal assets.
If the costs of a lawsuit go over your policy's limit,
an **umbrella policy** starts paying.

Umbrella policies, designed for both individuals and
businesses, were first written to serve two major functions:

- to provide **high limits** of coverage to
  protect against catastrophic losses; and

- to provide **broader** coverage than underlying policies.

**An umbrella policy will protect you if someone
sues you.**

Typically, these policies are purchased by high paid
professionals like executives, doctors, dentists, attor-
neys, etc. But don't assume that you don't need this
coverage. Lawsuits are constantly increasing in fre-
quency and severity.

An umbrella policy is written to provide you with
liability insurance on an **excess** basis, above underlying insurance or a **self-insured retention** (a layer
of losses absorbed by you).

The amount of this coverage usually ranges between
$1 million and $10 million.

Umbrella policies are not standard contracts and vary depending on the insurer. Some umbrellas are written to "follow form," meaning they don't provide broader coverage than the primary insurance. However, many are written to fill coverage gaps by providing coverages not included in the underlying insurance.

For losses that are covered by your primary policy, the umbrella coverage would begin to kick in only after the primary coverage is exhausted by payment of the **per occurrence** or **aggregate limit**. For losses that are covered by the umbrella and not by the primary policy, the umbrella coverage begins to apply after a loss exceeds an amount which the insured has agreed to retain.

The intent is to provide affordable, comprehensive coverage in case of a catastrophic loss, incidental exposure, and a modest gap in coverage, but not to provide blanket all-risk coverage in multiple areas where there is no primary insurance. For this reason, underwriters usually require an adequate range of underlying coverages for known exposures (personal liability, automobile liability, etc.), before providing you with umbrella coverage.

To a certain degree, the exclusions and limitations of an umbrella often follow the underlying policies. However, the umbrella will usually have fewer exclusions than the primary coverage, less restrictive exclusions, and a broader insuring agreement.

> A consistent problem with umbrella coverage is that policyholders try to use it as a cure-all for insurance problems. Umbrella coverage doesn't protect you from every risk in the world—it is excess insurance for whatever primary liability policies you have.

An umbrella policy offers a broader coverage than your homeowners policy. In addition to bodily injury and property damage, an umbrella policy covers false arrest, wrongful eviction, libel, slander, defamation of character and invasion of privacy.

PERSONAL UMBRELLA LIABILITY POLICY

Before your personal liability policy goes into effect, your insurer will typically require that all known major exposures be covered by any underlying policies that you may have and that each major exposure is declared in the umbrella policy with a premium shown.

For example, most people are required to have automobile insurance and a homeowners policy for family automobiles and the residence exposure. These exposures must be declared in your umbrella policy.

> If you own a boat and it is not declared, there will be no umbrella coverage for the boat exposure even if it is covered by an underlying boatowners policy.

The declarations also show the total policy premium and the limit of liability that applies. For example, if a limit of $500,000 is shown for umbrella coverage, that is the amount of insurance being provided in excess of the underlying coverages.

If the insured maintains underlying auto insurance on a **split limit basis**, then the deductible amount applicable to auto liability will be $250,000/$500,000 bodily injury and $25,000 property damage.

Types of Liability	Deductible Amounts Per Occurrence
Auto	$300,000
Personal	100,000
Recreational Motor Vehicles	100,000
Watercraft	100,000
Business Property	100,000
Business Pursuits	100,000
Employers Liability (where Workers' Compensation is required by law)	100,000
Loss Assessment	50,000

These limits are the minimum underlying limits for various required coverages. Automobiles must usually be insured for a single limit of at least $300,000 per occurrence (split limits are also permitted).

Most other exposures must be insured for a limit of at least $100,000.

> Note: The umbrella policy will only pay amounts in excess of these limits even if the underlying company becomes bankrupt or insolvent. An example: If you are held liable for $350,000 in damages resulting from an automobile accident and the auto insurance company becomes bankrupt, the umbrella policy will only cover $50,000 of the loss (the amount in excess of the deductible).

A special $1,000 deductible amount (also known as a "self-insured retention") applies to claims arising out of exposures which are covered by the umbrella policy but are not covered by the underlying insurance for some reason.

> An example: You're using your car and utility trailer to haul two large and valuable pieces of furniture for a friend. An accident occurs, the furniture is destroyed, and the friend sues for damages. Your personal auto policy excludes coverage for property being transported by you, but there is no such exclusion in the umbrella policy. This loss would be covered by the umbrella and the $1,000 deductible would apply.

An umbrella policy provides coverage on an excess basis for personal injury liability and property damage liability.

PERSONAL INJURY LIABILITY

Under an umbrella policy, the term "occurrence" means an accident, but it also includes continuous or repeated exposure to the same conditions. An example: An underground pipe on your property breaks and water seeps into your neighbor's yard over a period of several weeks. Eventually this causes collapse of a tool shed. The damage is treated as one occurrence.

For personal injury coverage (libel, slander, etc.) the term "occurrence" means an offense or series of related offenses. Libeling the same tenant in front of others on various occasions would be treated as a single occurrence if a personal injury claim were made. Since the offenses were related, the limit of insurance would not apply separately to each offense.

The **personal injury liability policy** covers your liability for personal injury. Personal injury includes bodily injury, sickness, disease, disability, shock, mental anguish and mental injury. The definition can also be extended to include: false arrest and imprisonment, wrongful entry or eviction, malicious prosecution or humiliation, libel, slander, defamation of character or invasion of privacy, and assault and battery not intentionally committed or directed by another insured.

If you commit any of the actions specified in this section, it could lead to a "personal injury" claim (notice that this term does not have the same meaning as bodily injury).

SPECIFIC LIABILITY ISSUES

False arrest claims are usually based on damage to a person's reputation when a suspected wrongdoer has been arrested without proper cause. False arrest may result from mistaken identity or an error in judgment. **False detention** or **imprisonment** restrict a person's freedom of movement, and can lead to a claim for damages.

Malicious prosecution generally occurs when a person brings charges against another without a probable cause to believe that the charges can be sustained, and there is a malicious intent in bringing the charges.

Libel is the defaming of another by writings, pictures or other publication which is injurious to the person's reputation. **Slander** is oral defamation of others which is injurious to their reputation. **Defamation** is the holding up of another to ridicule, and includes libel and slander.

Invasion of privacy is the publicizing of another's private affairs for which there is no legitimate public purpose, or the invasion into another's private activities which causes shame or humiliation to that person. **Wrongful eviction** is depriving a tenant of land or rental property by unjust, reckless or unfair means. **Wrongful entry** is the resumption of possession (repossession of real estate) by an owner or landlord of real property by unjust, reckless or unfair means.

PROPERTY DAMAGE LI-ABILITY

Under a property damage liability policy, your insurance company pays for personal injury or property damage for which you are legally liable and which exceeds the **retained limit**.

A retained limit can be either:

- the total applicable limits of all required underlying contracts and any other insurance available to an insured, or

- the self-insured retention if the loss is not covered by any underlying insurance.

Property damage means physical injury to, destruction of, or loss of use of tangible property.

Property damage includes loss of use. If you damage your neighbor's home, your neighbor might have to live somewhere else while the home is being repaired or rebuilt. The extra expenses for loss of use (rent, meals, transportation) could be claimed in addition to the actual damages to the home.

WHO'S INSURED UNDER AN UMBRELLA

An umbrella policy will cover you on an excess basis while using a non-owned auto, only if the use of that auto is covered by underlying insurance.

An example: You work for the Ajax Company, which provides you with a car for use in your sales work. As long as your employer's policy provides at least $300,000 of coverage for your use of the company-owned car, your umbrella policy will provide additional coverage.

Family members are insured for their use of owned autos, or autos furnished for their regular use, only if their use of such autos is covered by the required underlying insurance.

Example: Mr. and Mrs. Jones have a personal umbrella policy and their teenage daughter lives with them. The daughter has her own car. The umbrella policy will cover the daughter's use of the car if she has personal auto coverage with a limit of at least $300,000.

For autos or boats owned or in your care, any other person using such items, or any person or organization responsible for the acts of someone using such items, would be insured.

If your son lets a friend drive the family speedboat, the friend would be considered an insured person. If he uses your boat to teach members of his son's Boy Scout troop to water ski, the Boy Scout troop would be considered an insured person.

For animals owned by any family member, any other person or organization responsible for the animals is an insured person.

An example: While on vacation, you leave the family dog with a neighbor who has agreed to take care of it. If the dog breaks loose and bites a jogger, the umbrella policy would cover the neighbor as an insured person if the neighbor is sued for the injury.

None of the following is considered an "insured" under this policy:

- the owner or lessor of an auto, recreational motor vehicle or watercraft loaned to or hired for use by an "insured" or on an "insured's" behalf;

- a person or organization having custody of animals owned by you or a family member in the course of any business or without the consent of an insured.

An example: If you rent a boat for fishing, the boat rental company will not be considered an insured person under this policy (it should have its own liability coverage).

Another example: If your daughter owns a horse which is boarded at Sunset Stables for a fee, the stable will not be considered an insured person under this policy (it should have its own liability coverage).

WHAT'S COVERED?

Umbrella policies provide **legal liability insurance**. This means that the coverage applies only if you're found to be legally responsible for one of the types of injury or damage insured against. Covered damages include pre-judgment interest.

> The duty to defend a claim ends when the insurance company has paid damages equal to its limit of liability.

If laws prevent the insurance company from defending you, it will pay expenses for defense which are incurred with its written consent.

In addition to the limit of liability, your insurance company pays:

1) All expenses incurred and costs taxed against an insured.

2) Premiums on required bonds, but not for bond amounts more than the limit of liability. You need not apply for or furnish any bond.

3) Reasonable expenses (other than loss of earnings) an insured incurs at the insurance company's request.

4) An insured's loss of earnings, but not other income, up to $100 per day, to attend trials or hearings.

When your insurer defends a claim or suit, it will pay all of its own expenses and reasonable expenses incurred by you at its request. But coverage for your loss of earnings while attending trials or hearings is limited to $100 a day. The insurer will also pay premiums for required bonds and post-judgment interest.

Your insurer will pay for your share of the **loss assessment** charged during the coverage period against you, as owner or tenant of the residence premises, by a corporation or association of property owners. The assessment must arise from an occurrence covered by the policy and applies only to assessments in excess of the "minimum retained limit."

If you're owner or tenant of a condominium unit, the umbrella policy will pay your share of loss assessments charged against you by the condominium association.

Loss assessments against individual unit owners are often made when the condominium association is held liable for a loss which exceeds the limits of its liability insurance, or is not covered by its policy.

EXCLUSIONS UNDER AN UMBRELLA

Exclusions appear in insurance policies to shape and limit the coverage to what is intended by the contract. In some cases, exclusions apply to exposures which are not insurable. In other cases, exclusions apply to exposures which should be covered by another kind of policy.

Coverage under an umbrella policy is excluded for an act committed by or at the direction of an insured with intent to cause bodily injury or property damage. This does not apply to bodily injury or property damage resulting from an act committed to protect persons or property, or to prevent or eliminate danger in the operation of an auto or watercraft.

Because insurance is designed to cover accidental and unexpected losses, intentional acts of an insured person are not covered. But a few exceptions are made for situations where an insured person acts with the intent of protecting persons, property, or preventing a greater loss.

An example: An injury caused by use of a weapon against a criminal who intends to rob and injure another would not be excluded.

Another example: If your car's brakes fail and you purposely drive the auto into a building in order to avoid hitting children crossing the street, the damage to the building would not be excluded.

UNLAWFUL ACTS

Personal injury losses resulting from an insured person breaking the law are excluded. The intent of this provision is similar to that of the exclusion of intentional acts.

Since this is a personal umbrella policy, business exposures are generally excluded, however, exceptions are made for incidental exposures, and for business exposures that are declared and covered.

Activities which are common non-business activities are covered, even if related to your business.

An example: While playing golf with a customer, an

insured salesman hits a long drive and the ball hits another golfer on an adjacent fairway and causes injury. This accident would not be excluded because playing golf is a "non-business" type of activity.

> No liability coverage is provided for a person who uses your vehicle or boat without reasonable authority to do so.

An example: If a person steals your boat and causes an accident, the thief would not be covered by the insured's umbrella policy if sued for damages (the insured would still be covered if sued as the owner).

Another example: If a neighbor has used your boat on numerous occasions, and has been told that it may be used whenever it is not being used by a family member, the neighbor would be insured for use of the boat. This is true even if an accident occurs at a time when you have no knowledge that the boat is being used.

The only racing exposure that is covered is sailboat racing. No coverage is provided for racing vehicles or motorized boats, or while practicing for such a race.

> Liability insurance is known as "third party" coverage, because it is designed to pay damages suffered by others when you are responsible. For this reason, injuries suffered by you or family members are not covered.

This provision was added in recent years following a number of claims for damages due to the transmission of diseases such as herpes and AIDS among family members. Some courts required insurance companies to pay these damages under personal liability policies. Liability arising out of the transmission of a communicable disease is now excluded.

Similarly, there is no coverage for property owned by you, or by an association of owners of which you are a member (such as the common property jointly owned by a condominium association). Coverage is also excluded for damage to property that is rented, used or occupied by you or in your care, but only to the extent that you have agreed to insure the property in a written agreement.

An example: You rent furniture and agree in the rental contract to insure it for a stipulated amount.

The umbrella policy will not provide coverage for that amount (it might provide some additional excess coverage). The property would be covered if there was no written agreement by you to provide other coverage (but the umbrella deductible will still apply).

A personal umbrella policy includes loss assessment coverage for owners of condominium units. When bodily injury, property damage, or personal injury occurs on the "common" premises (not within any owner's unit), a claim for damages may be made against the association. If the loss is not covered by or exceeds the limits of the association's liability policy, it would be necessary for the association to assess the individual owners for a proportionate amount of the loss.

For this coverage, the term *occurrence* has the same meaning as it does for other liability coverages, except that it also includes acts of directors, officers, or trustees of the association.

> **Note: If you are serving as an officer of a corporation or member of a board of directors, your acts are generally excluded from coverage because this is a professional liability exposure. But coverage is provided if you're acting for a nonprofit organization and receive no pay for services.**

While the policy will cover some loss assessments made by organizations such as condominium associations, it will not cover assessments made by a governmental body against you or the association, nor will it cover an assessment made by the association to pay for a deductible which applies to an underlying policy.

LIMITS TO WHAT THE POLICY WILL COVER

Your insurer's total liability under your umbrella policy for all damages and loss assessments resulting from any one occurrence will not be more than the limit of liability as shown in the Declarations. The limit is the same regardless of the number of insureds, claims made, loss assessments, persons injured, vehicles involved in an accident, or exposures or premiums shown in the Declarations.

Should two or more insureds, such as you and another family member, be sued, the policy will provide a defense for each insured. However, the limit of liability for all damages arising out of one occurrence remains unchanged.

An insurance company is entitled to appeal any judgment which could result in a claim payment being made under the umbrella policy. This is true even if you or your insurance company providing underlying insurance elects not to appeal the judgment. If it appeals, the insurance company will pay all costs related to the appeal.

If you become bankrupt, the umbrella policy still applies on an excess basis over the applicable deductibles. The umbrella will not become primary coverage due to a lack of underlying insurance or your inability to pay the deductible.

CONCLUSION

If you are in need of broader coverage than what your homeowners policy has to offer, you may want to consider an umbrella policy which provides separate coverage over and above any underlying insurance that you may have.

Chapter 7 will discuss inland marine insurance.

HOW INLAND MARINE INSURANCE WORKS

Houses can't be moved (well, not without a lot of expense). Because of this, the perils to which a house will be subject are limited. But, you own other types of property that can be moved and subjected to perils other than those pertaining to stationary property (such as transportation perils) and to an increased risk of other perils (such as theft).

The contents coverage provided by your homeowners policy is meant to cover average personal property exposures which don't have special value.

This includes such things as furnishings, clothing, household appliances and many other personal possessions found in a typical home.

Some property (such as jewelry and furs, and items that are made of gold or silver), however, can have special value due to intrinsic factors. And other property (such as antiques and collectibles) can have special value due to market value factors.

Sometimes, property of this nature is also more susceptible to certain perils (for example, collectible porcelains or other fragile antiques to the peril of breakage). Such risks are insured under **inland marine insurance.**

The term "inland marine" relates to property which has special coverage needs for one or both of the following reasons:

- it is mobile; and

- its value is intrinsic or market-driven.

In much the same way that current homeowners policies have their roots in an older class of coverage (fire insurance), inland marine insurance finds its roots in an even older line — ocean marine insurance. At one time, ocean transportation was the primary mode of moving goods from one point to another. Ocean marine insurers provided coverage for ships and cargo, and became quite experienced in dealing with transportation perils.

With the rise of other transportation systems (railroads, motor vehicles and, eventually, air carriers), their was a growing need for insurance to cover these risks. Insurers began marketing policies that provided coverage for property while being transported on a wide variety of conveyances, and for a very broad range of perils. They also began selling policies that covered property having a special value.

Originally, marine coverage began and ended at the ports of origin and destination. But, as warehouses moved further and further inland, insurers began providing coverage for property even while it was stored at these warehouses. At this point they strayed into an area which historically had been the domain of fire and casualty insurers. The fire and casualty insurers objected because property in storage had only an incidental relationship to transportation.

This conflict inspired the National Association of Insurance Commissioners (NAIC) to develop a nationwide marine definition, describing the risks that are covered by marine policies. The categories are actually very broad, including many kinds of imports, exports, domestic shipments, instruments of transportation and communication (ranging from bridges and tunnels to pipelines and powerlines) and both personal and commercial property floater risks (which includes most kinds of property which can be moved from one point to another).

A homeowners policy recognizes that you own special classes of personal property; but, since the coverage (and rates) are designed to cover average risks, limitations apply to the coverage. Without additional insurance, you may not be adequately covered for special classes of personal property which have a unique value or a unique exposure to loss.

Personal property coverage under the broad and special homeowners policies is also limited to the broad form perils which can result in uninsured losses (for example, breakage of fragile items).

Loss valuation is also important. A homeowners policy values personal property at actual cash value at the time of loss, but many special classes of property have values which are not adequately represented by the traditional definition of ACV.

INLAND MARINE COVERAGE FORMS

Inland marine forms may provide limits of coverage in three formats to cover the gaps in your homeowners policy:

- Scheduled coverage (individually declared items and values)
- Blanket coverage (a stated value to cover everything in a given class)
- A combination of scheduled and blanket coverage

Jewelry, fine art and cameras are examples of property usually covered on a scheduled basis. In contrast, floaters covering personal effects or wedding presents are typically written on a blanket basis. Stamp and coin floaters can be a combination of both (a blanket amount for the entire collection, with scheduled amounts for individual items).

Inland marine floaters have the following features:

- coverage written on a risks-of-direct-loss approach ("all-risk" instead of named perils);
- "floating" nature of coverage (coverage applies anywhere within the stated policy territory, which is typically worldwide, except that fine art is limited to the U. S. and Canada);
- versatility of coverage (insureds may select only those classes of property for

which they desire coverage, and also select a predetermined limit for each coverage).

This chapter will review a number of inland marine floaters and discuss several special classes of property that may be insured, such as sports memorabilia, large coin or stamp collections, large antique or art collections and sports equipment.

INSURING AGREEMENT

The first sentence on the first page of a **scheduled personal property endorsement** is an insuring agreement. For an additional premium, coverage is provided for the classes of property for which an amount of insurance is shown. A homeowners policy property insurance deductible will not apply to this coverage.

Here are some examples of how personal property endorsements work and what they cover.

Jewelry: This class is not described, except to say that it means jewelry "as scheduled" in the endorsement.

Furs: This class includes garments trimmed with fur or consisting principally of fur. So, a leather coat with a fox fur collar could be scheduled here as a fur item (the entire coat).

Cameras: This class includes projectors, film and "related articles of equipment." This wording is broad enough to cover things like darkroom equipment. Additionally, there is no limitation on professional usage as is found in the next class (musical instruments).

Musical instruments: This class also includes "related articles of equipment." In today's electronic music world, this can cover amplifiers, mike stands and other equipment.

> The description of this class also contains a stipulation on the coverage: You agree not to perform with these instruments for pay unless specifically provided under this policy. This prohibits professional use (such as playing at wedding receptions for pay), unless the insurer has agreed in advance. (In which case it will probably charge an additional premium.)

Silverware: This class includes silverware, silver-plated ware, goldware, gold-plated ware, and pewterware. However, certain types of goods aren't meant to be included in this class. It does not include pens, pencils, flasks, smoking implements (low value items which are undesirable from an underwriting standpoint) and jewelry (which is covered under another class).

Golf equipment: This class includes golf clubs, clothing and equipment. Does this mean that even golf balls are covered? Yes, but a later condition of coverage limits the perils for which that coverage is provided. Additionally, coverage is generally provided on a blanket basis.

Fine art: This class includes fine art "as scheduled." However, the premium for this coverage is based on the insured's statement that the property insured is located at a specified address. (The address must be shown in the schedule.) An optional coverage is also offered under the fine art section—coverage for breakage of fragile items. For an additional premium, an exclusion concerning breakage will not apply to specified items.

Postage stamps and rare and current coins: These classes of property are not described beyond this.

Additional items may be scheduled by description and amount of insurance. This is considered an **open class**, because anything the insurer is willing to accept may be scheduled there.

COVERED PERILS

Since coverage is provided on an all-risk basis, the exclusions of an inland marine policy play an important role in shaping coverage. Generally, the endorsement contains four exclusions:

- wear and tear, gradual deterioration, or inherent vice;
- insects or vermin;
- war or any warlike act; and
- nuclear hazard.

Note: A fifth exclusion applies only to fine art. These are special perils to which fine art can be particularly susceptible—damage done during repair, restoration, or retouching, or breakage to art glass windows, glassware, statuary, marble, bric-a-brac, porcelains and similar fragile articles. (Coverage is given back for breakage if caused by a specified peril.)

"All risk" coverage provided by this endorsement is broader than similar types of property insurance forms which don't include breakage coverage, for earthquakes and floods.

> Coverage is not provided for loss to any property on exhibition at fair grounds or premises of national or international expositions unless the premises are covered by a policy. However, if an insured loans items to a museum, or to be put on display at a local mall, there would be coverage.

A final set of exclusions applies only to postage stamps and rare or current coin collections.

Some of these relate to perils to which the items are particularly susceptible—fading, tearing, transfer of colors, inherent defect, damage while being handled or worked on—and therefore are uninsurable.

SPECIAL PROVISIONS

Due to the special nature of some of the classes of scheduled personal property, a few special provisions apply:

Fine arts—competent packers. Some types of fine arts are very fragile and may be easily damaged due to what they are made of, or how they are constructed. Therefore, a condition stipulates that when and if you transport such items, they will be handled by competent packers.

Golf equipment. Here we find a slight broadening of this coverage stating that it is extended to include the clothes you store in a locker while you are playing golf. There is coverage for the loss of golf balls by the perils of fire and burglary, and for a burglary loss to be covered there must be visible evidence of forcible entry into a building, room or locker.

Postage stamps. This provision describes the various types of stamps and other philatelic property owned by you or in your custody or control which may be insured. This class includes property such as books, mounting pages, and the like.

Rare and current coins. Property insured under the class of coin collections may include medals, paper money, bank notes, tokens and other numismatic property, including coin albums, containers, frames, and even display cases used with such collections.

CONDITIONS

Just as any policy, an inland marine policy has conditions which state the rights and duties of both you and your insurer. Here are just a few:

Loss clause. If the total loss of a scheduled article occurs, the remaining amount of insurance for all property of that class will be reduced by the amount of the item lost. Provision is then made for the refund of the unearned premium applicable to the lost item for the remainder of the policy term.

Example: An insured has $20,000 of blanket coverage for a rare coin collection. One particular rare coin, covered for a scheduled amount of $3,000 is lost, and the insurer pays the $3,000 claim. The remaining coverage for the coin collection is then reduced to $17,000—an amount which reflects the remaining exposure.

Loss settlement. This may easily be the most misunderstood area involving scheduled personal property coverage. It is important to understand that loss valuation applies differently to different types of property.

Fine art. This is the only class of property for which agreed amount coverage applies. If there is a total loss of any scheduled item, the insurer will pay the amount shown as the scheduled value in the Declarations. If partial loss occurs to a pair or set, the total declared value will be paid, and the insured must surrender the remaining part of the set to the insurer.

Stamp and coin collections. Valuation of loss for stamp or coin collections depends upon how the coverage is written. In the case of items which are insured for scheduled amounts, losses will be paid in accordance with the provisions that apply to "other property" (the next valuation method described in the endorsement). In the case of items which are covered on a blanket basis (unscheduled items), the insurer will pay up to the market value at the time of loss, but not more than $250 for any one stamp, coin or individual article, and not more than $1,000 for any unscheduled coin collection. However, if the class of property is underinsured, the insurer will not pay more than the proportion that the blanket amount bears to the market value. (In other words, if an insured carries $10,000 of blanket coverage for collections that have an actual market value of $20,000 at the time of loss, the insurer will pay half of any covered loss.)

Other property. For all other property, including scheduled stamps and coins, the value is not an agreed amount, but will be determined at the time of loss. Despite the fact that a scheduled amount is shown, the insurer will not pay more than the lesser of the following amounts: the actual cash value, the reasonable cost to repair the property to its prior condition, the reasonable cost to replace property with substantially identical property, or the scheduled amount of insurance. This means that a scheduled amount is not necessarily the amount paid for a loss—but it could be paid if it is less than the alternative amounts (ACV, repair or replacement cost).

LOSS TO A PAIR OR SET

Pair, set or parts other than fine art. This final condition is a pair and set clause that applies to all property other than fine art. In essence, it states that if there is a loss to a pair or set, the insurer has the option of paying the repair or replacement cost to restore the value of the pair or set to its pre-loss value, or of paying the difference between pre-loss and post-loss actual cash value. In the case of loss to any part of property consisting of several parts, the insurer will pay for the value of the part lost or damaged.

Premiums for certain classes of property may be lowered if you attempt to protect your property from loss. So, if you normally keep your jewelry in a vault, you may have significantly lower rates than if you kept the jewelry at home.

Many classes of inland marine property—especially small, high value items, which are easily stolen are particularly susceptible to losses by moral or morale hazard. Consequently, an insured strapped for cash could conceivably look to "liquidate" some of his or her scheduled property to cash in on the insurance proceeds.

If you are thinking of doing this, you may want to think again. Even if you don't realize it, your insurer may be aware of your actions. If you have a low income, and suddenly request significant amounts of scheduled coverage for jewelry or fine art, keep in mind, that this is enough to draw the attention of your insurer (even if you are being honest).

PERSONAL EFFECTS FLOATER

Personal effects floaters (PEFs), which are discussed in more detail in Chapter 5, are traditionally used by travelers who desire broad coverage for personal property on an extended vacation. Because of this, they are technically considered forms of inland marine insurance.

A PEF covers **personal effects** that are carried by tourists and travelers, including items used or worn by you and your family. Typically, a PEF covers shoes, clothing, luggage, cameras, and many other personal possessions.

Exclusions and limitations are used to narrow the coverage in some areas for losses which are difficult to prove and which could cause underwriting concerns if the coverage were provided. For example, no coverage is provided for money and transportation tickets — these items are often subject to other-than-fortuitous losses (loss by carelessness, or even false claims of loss). Additionally, certain types of property are limited to only minimal amounts of coverage ($100 per article for loss of jewelry, watches, silver and gold items, or furs).

> One interesting exclusion states that no coverage is provided for personal effects while on the premises where the insured normally lives, or while in storage. This clarifies the intent that coverage is only provided while an insured is actually away on vacation.

ELECTRONIC DATA PROCESSING FLOATER

The need for **personal computer insurance** has increased in direct proportion to the rising popularity of home computers. Today, there are tens of millions of personal computers in use in the United States, and sales continue to increase each year.

Computer equipment is expensive, and it is relatively easy to transport. Although desktop systems are not as easily moved around as the portable laptop PCs, any thief who could steal a T.V. could make off with computer equipment.

> Theft is the leading cause of computer losses. Computers are susceptible to loss by many of the same perils as other property (such as fire, lightning and theft), but they are also susceptible to loss or damage by some unique perils (such as power surge, and mechanical breakdown).

Insurance Services Office (ISO) homeowners policies provide some coverage for personal computers, but do not cover any disks or media containing business data, and do not cover any damage caused by power surge. If a personal computer is used for any business purposes, an ISO homeowners policy limits coverage to $2,500 while on the premises. Some forms don't cover home computers at all if they are used for business.

The limitations on covered perils and business exposures create a need for special personal computer coverage. Many home computers are used for some business purposes, which means that business data is not protected by a homeowners policy. The dollar limitations are easily exceeded if an individual owns a high-end personal computer, an expensive laser printer, and commercial software programs. Even if you don't have any business exposures, you may desire computer coverage beyond what is provided by a homeowners policy.

Extensive computer coverage is available under stand-alone policies issued by specialty carriers as well as endorsements to standard homeowners policies. Many of these forms are considered to be inland marine forms.

Coverage is provided on an all-risk basis, but some exclusions specifically address computer-related exposures. Here are some features of the policy:

- Coverage is provided for business property (business use does not invalidate the insurance).

- Scheduled computer hardware is covered (this means the computer itself and related equipment, such as printers, modems and connecting cables).

- Scheduled media is covered (this means the material on which data is stored, such as hard disks, floppy disks and tape backup systems).

- Scheduled data is covered (this means data stored on media which is available from a commercial source, such as commercial software programs; coverage for any other non-commercial data, including any programs developed by the insured, is limited to $250).

- Coverage is provided for newly acquired property of a type listed in the schedule, subject to a limit of 25 percent of the amount of insurance shown for the class of property or $1,000, whichever is less. (The insured must report this new property within 30 days and pay an additional premium.)

Besides the exclusions for earthquakes, floods, war and nuclear hazards, the coverage is narrowed by computer-specific exclusions:

- mechanical breakdown or failure;

- damage caused by any repair process;

- erasure of data, unless caused by lightning;

- computer fraud.

> Mechanical breakdown coverage is available through the specialty market. (These policies may be thought of as "extended warranty" or "repair and maintenance" contracts.) Earthquake coverage for computers is also available through the specialty market.

PARTICIPATING POLICIES

Two or more companies may participate in covering a risk where the schedule is identical on all policies, but each company must show its agreed percentage of the total coverage. It is permissible, also, for two or more companies to divide a risk by insuring different articles for the full amount; but in such cases, full rates are applied to whatever values are to be insured.

> Inland Marine coverages may be included with other policies (such as homeowners policies), provided that the supplemental endorsement which provides the coverage includes all the terms, conditions, rules and minimum premiums applicable to the particular floater coverage being attached.

The premium payment plan, the attachment provision and the cancellation provisions, however, may be the same as those of the policy to which the floater coverage is attached.

MORE FLOATERS

You can usually find coverage for physical loss to your bicycles (as long as the damage exceeds $5) under an inland marine policy. Coverage applies if you live in the Continental United States, Canada, Hawaii and Puerto Rico.

> Motor bicycles or any other motor-powered conveyances are not covered under an inland marine policy.

Coverage does not apply to your bicycles for any wear, tear, inherent vice, deterioration, rust, mechanical breakdown or derangement, loss by any process or while property is being worked on, unless loss is caused by fire or explosion, war and nuclear hazards, except loss by fire resulting from nuclear hazard is covered.

Coverage for boats also can be written under inland marine forms. The coverage provided on the hull is similar to that provided in yacht policies.

Inland marine will cover you for worldwide physical loss to the following items under the class of cameras and projection machines:

- Scheduled cameras, projection machines and relevant articles of equipment.

- Movable sound equipment pertaining to the recording, projection, reproduction, and operation of motion pictures.

- Home video cameras, playback recorders and relevant articles of equipment.

- Miscellaneous property such as films, binoculars, telescopes, microscopes and the like, which are used in conjunction with cameras or photographic equipment.

This coverage does not apply to television cameras and equipment, and coin or token operated devices, cameras or camera property belonging to dealers or manufacturers, and aerial cameras or radar cameras.

If you are using a camera that does not belong to you—it belongs to your employer or you are renting the equipment—you may want to check out coverage for camera and related equipment owned by many commercial enterprises. Business policies have braod coverage.

Newly acquired property is covered up to 25 percent of the aggregate amount insured (or $10,000, whichever is less) subject to reporting within 30 days and paying the applicable pro rata premium. These limits may be set at lower amounts at the insurance company's discretion.

CONVENTIONS, TOURS, ETC.

Policies may be issued covering conventions, tours, trade shows, etc. provided each individual to be insured is named together with the amount of insurance applicable to each.

An exclusion relating to students' property in fraternities, sororities, dormitories, etc., may be waived for an additional premium of $.25 per $100 on the total amount insured, but not less than $5 per annum, subject to short rate for short term.

CONCLUSION

This chapter has gone over the major coverages available to you for property that is mobile. If you are interested in learning more about floater policies turn to Chapter 5 of this book.

In the next chapter we will discuss the various specialty and customized insurance coverages that are available through many insurance companies.

CHAPTER 8

SPECIALTY AND CUSTOMIZED INSURANCE

Some personal possessions are generally not covered or are covered insufficiently under homeowners insurance policies because they don't fit the standard definition of risk that most insurers have selected to insure.

If you are having trouble finding coverage for that one particular item, you may want to ask your agent what type of specialty lines your insurer has to offer.

With a **special coverage form**, you can insure your items on an open perils, all-risk basis. These forms provide the broadest coverage and do not list covered perils, but do include a lengthy list of exclusions. This chapter, will consider a few types of specialty coverage that most specialty lines insurers offer.

COLLECTIONS

Today, we live in a society with a thriving subculture that treasures and collects things like Flintstones lunch boxes, eight-track tapes, spider-man comic books and

Barbie doll wardrobes. We may not know what drives people to collect Hot Wheels matchbox cars or "Donny and Marie" dolls. But we do know that these items are some of today's most valuable collectibles—and they aren't in museums, but in the closets of ordinary people with not so ordinary insurable needs.

With conventions built around the sale and trade of these items, insurers are responding and writing out policies for this property.

Insurance companies usually offer coverage for collections of all values on an all-risk basis, including flood, earthquake, fire, theft and breakage. Generally, collections are specifically tailored for collectors and described based on recent price guides, recently documented sales, auction offerings or by experts in the field of your collection.

Ask your homeowner or rental insurance carrier about finding insurance for your collections. Today, coverage for these items is pretty easy to get—in fact, many insurance companies even offer **pop collectibles** coverage riders.

Depending on the value of your collection, you may be required to take certain measures to secure the premises at which your collection is stored. As discussed in other chapters, you may also want to photograph your collection—especially items of high value. And be sure to store these items in a safe place (usually off the premises).

Do you own any of the following?

- records, tapes, CDs;

- record awards;

- sheet music;

- original concert posters and handbills;

- original movie posters;

- photographs;

- promotional items; or

- other collectible music and entertainment memorabilia.

If you're looking to insure the collection of blues albums that your insurer won't cover, you may want to look into specialty coverage for the collection.

COVERAGE FOR FINE ART COLLECTIONS

Under a **fine art collection policy** you will be covered for loss due to breakage of items but this is limited for fragile articles such as glassware, statuary, marble, etc.

A fine art collection policy will insure you against all risks of physical loss to the covered property, not including coverage for typical wear and tear, deterioration, insects, etc.

Perils insured against include fire, lightning, aircraft, windstorm, malicious damage, theft, explosion, earthquake, flood, collision, derailment or overturn of conveyance.

> If you are having art restored or repaired, you won't be covered for any damages during the process.

Any newly acquired art will be covered for its actual cash value, up to 25 percent of the amount of the existing insurance—but only for 90 days.

> Unless the premises at where you are displaying your art has insurance, you won't be covered for any loss while your property is on exhibition.

If there is a loss to a pair or set of your collection, your insurance company will pay the full scheduled amount for the value of the pair or set as long as you turn over the undamaged portion to the company.

> If damage to your expensive fur occurred while it was being mended at the furriers—you may find coverage under your furrier's *specialty line furriers customers insurance.* Ask your insurer for more details on this kind of coverage.

TRIP CANCELLATION

Here's something else you may want to think about purchasing insurance for—trip cancellation.

If you've been saving up for five years to take your dream vacation, and something goes wrong, you may want to have **trip cancellation insurance** (TCI) to protect you for the full or partial loss of any payment made toward a major package tour or cruise.

For example: The Green family contacts a tour operator who signs them up for a $4,000 vacation package including: airfare, lodging, a car and Disney World passes. But, the tour operator wants the payment for their trip in full and months in advance. These types of deals are usually non-refundable, so it would make sense for this family to purchase a policy for around $200 to protect the whole package.

> For less than $500 a TCI can provide you with peace of mind if you booked a fairly expensive trip or cruise.

Typically, there are two types of TCI policies. **Custom** policies let you choose your own coverage from a selection of options. This type of policy is generally more expensive—ranging from about $4 to $7 per $100 of the total of the trip.

Cruise/tour coverage typically offers a selection of coverages with a price based on the total cost of the trip. These are generally cheaper than the custom policies because they are standardized.

The most important areas of coverage in a travel-insurance policy include:

- **Illness, injury or death**. This coverage would protect you against any losses caused by personal mishaps—or if you have to cancel the trip due to illness, injury or death of a close family member.

- **Pre-existing conditions**. Some policies exclude coverage for any interruption or cancellation of a trip due to a medical problem that arose 60 days before you purchased the policy. However, if you have a condition that is controlled by medication, this would be covered. Other insurers will not cover any pre-existing condition that required treatment or medical advice within 90 to 180 days of buying the policy. (Some companies will waive these limitations if you buy a TCI for the full values of your trip one to seven days after you make the first deposit on the trip.)

- **Emergency medical evacuation**. This coverage pays for whatever transportation is required to get you home.

- **Operator failure**. This is the most important trip coverage to have. It will pay if your tour operator fails, defaults or ceases operations.

Beware of policies that only offer coverage if a tour operator goes bankrupt. They won't cover you if he decides to take off with your first three payments.

- **Home problems** and **destination ca-lamities**. Trip-cancellation insurance will also cover you against a number of misfortunes and surprises at your home or destination that might cause you to cancel or interrupt your trip.

Don't overbuy. If you insure your trip for more than the amount at risk, your coverage will be pointless.

PLANNING A WEDDING?

If you are, you should know that the average cost of a wedding is around $16,000. An amount that many agree is worth insuring.

Insurance is probably the last thing on your mind but, you may want to consider coverage to guard against losing unrefundable deposits to the businesses and vendors who are involved with your wedding.

If death, illness, or some other disaster cause cancellation on their part—you could be left without the flowers, the cake—maybe even the wedding dress.

Check your homeowners policy it may already provide you with coverage. You can also purchase floaters for things like wedding presents. (More on wedding presents in Chapter 5.)

It doesn't hurt to check out the business' or vendor's policy either. Sometimes their business policies will cover you for a loss on their part.

Are you covered if Uncle Leo has a little too much to drink at your reception or after-reception party? You may want to look into this coverage—some courts have found hosts responsible for the damage caused by their drunken guests.

INSURING YOUR PET

If you have a cat, and your insurance company doesn't provide you with coverage for it you might want to look for coverage elsewhere.

There are some policies that will pay on claims made for death benefit, loss of cat, legal liability or even high-priced vet fees.

Normally paid in a pre-determined lump sum, some insurers offer a **death benefit** if your cat dies following an accident or injury. However, it might not apply if Whiskers is an older cat.

The policy may also cover you in the event that your cat is stolen or strays away from home. If so, the policy will usually have a defined period for the cat to be found before any payment can be made.

You may even be covered for the cost of advertising and offering a reward for the recovery of your cat under this policy.

LIABILITY AND THOSE OTHER VEHICLES

The greatest exposure to liability loss that you face from a personal standpoint is the personal auto exposure. Given the number of cars careening past one another daily on America's streets and highways, its a wonder there aren't more accidents than there are.

Still, a fondness for motorized transportation has developed several spin-off modes of motorized travel. Some are designed for travel on those same public highways, while some are simply for off-road fun. Nonetheless, they too have the potential for causing injury to someone or damage to their property. And due to the nature of these vehicles, they can also present hazards that do not exist for the operator of a typical private passenger auto. Additionally, these vehicles can cost thousands of dollars—a significant property loss for you should damage or destruction of the vehicle occur.

The following is a list of vehicles that generally find coverage under a specialty policy.

Two-wheeled vehicles: The vehicles most commonly thought of when the term "recreational vehicles" is used are motorcycles. They are subject to motor vehicle registration. Since they operate on the street, they subject the owner and operator to many of the same exposures as a private passenger auto. However, they introduce some additional hazards—they can accelerate rapidly and are capable of high speeds; due to their size, they are sometimes hard to see by other motorists. The following are four types of two-wheeled vehicles:

- *Traditional motorcycles*—which are designed for street use and are subject to motor vehicle registration

- *Mini-bikes*—small low speed vehicles, generally used off road, consisting of not much more than a lawnmower engine with a frame around it and a seat over it

- *Dirt bikes* (sometimes called trail bikes)—vehicles, like small motorcycles, designed for off road use on trails or in the woods, and can be very fast

- *Mopeds*—these vehicles are simply bicycles with a motor, which the user pedals to start, and do not have much speed capability. (IMPORTANT: some states or localities subject mopeds to motor vehicle registration as a class of motorcycle.)

OTHER VEHICLES

Motor homes: These large, self-propelled vehicles are usually quite expensive, which creates a significant property exposure for the owner. Motor homes are designed for use on public roads and are subject to registration. They also are quite different to drive than a regular auto, and some operators of motor homes encounter difficulty even while driving them on the open road. This creates an increased potential for liability losses especially if the driver is inexperienced.

Camper trailers: This is another class of specialty vehicle that comes in a variety of sizes and styles, from economical pop-up tent campers to massive, very expensive fifth-wheel trailers which are close in size to a mobile home.

All terrain vehicles (ATVs): This class may include three-wheeled or four-wheeled, off-road vehicles with oversized tires designed for travel over different types of terrain. They may be driven on public roads, but they are designed for off road use and are not subject to motor vehicle registration.

Golf carts: These vehicles may be electric or gas powered, may have three or four wheels, and are designed to carry one or two people and their golfing equipment. While usually operated on the golf course, they are sometimes used in retirement communities as transportation to and from the golf course, or even to run local errands such as picking up groceries. Golf carts can represent a serious liability exposure if they are being used off of the golf course and are covered only by Section II of a homeowners policy.

Snowmobiles: A snowmobile is a popular type of specialty vehicle that has no wheels at all. These vehicles are commonly used for recreation and transportation in parts of the country where there is snow on the ground for a number of months during the year. Snowmobiles are powered by gas engines which drive a track or belt that provides forward motion. The body of a snowmobile rests on skis, located at the front of the unit, which are used for steering. Snowmobiles may have room for an operator or an operator and one or more passengers. These units are generally operated off roads and can achieve significant speeds. Snowmobiles require a different level of operating skill than other types of off-road vehicles.

Dune buggies: A dune buggy is another type of specialty vehicle. You've probably seen one before, even if you don't live near the beach or the desert. These vehicles are little more than a car-sized frame and engine, and have oversized tires for driving on sand.

Very limited coverage for these vehicles can be provided by unendorsed ISO homeowners and personal auto policies. However, specialty policies also can cover such vehicles.

Independently filed forms are available, but insurers change them periodically for competitive reasons. With such variation, the best approach is to read some of the available policies, compare them to ISO coverage forms, and decide which policy best fits your needs.

SPECIALTY COVERAGE

When it comes to specialty vehicles, insurers typically will insure you for such things as:

- **Vacation expense coverage.** This coverage partially offsets the extra expense an insured may encounter if a loss causes the motor vehicle (motor home or travel trailer) to become unusable, forcing the insured to bear the unexpected expenses of hotel lodging and/or restaurant meals.

- **Road service coverage.** Some specialty policies for motor homes include road service coverage, which is similar to the towing coverage available under the personal auto policy (PAP). Such coverage is provided at significantly higher limits than towing would be under the PAP, as the average cost of towing a large motor home is substantially higher than towing a private passenger auto.

- **Motor home furnishings.** Some policies covering motor homes or travel trailers provide coverage for personal property and furnishings used in connection with the motor home or trailer.

- **Snowmobile racing.** Some snowmobile policies will provide restricted physical damage coverage for informal racing activities, at a higher premium and increased deductible

- **Motorcycle coverage.** Under specialty policies motorcycle coverage is usually provided on an a la carte basis, starting with a basic liability package and making additional coverages available. Among these you may find guest liability (similar in purpose to not excluding the passenger hazard under a miscellaneous type vehicle endorsement).

Another aspect of some independently filed forms is a provision for lay up time. Many vehicles of the types we have discussed have a prime operating time of year, and conversely a portion of the year in which usage of the vehicle (such as snowmobiles), is unlikely or impossible. These policies can suspend all but other-than-collision coverage for the time period in which the vehicle probably won't be used, at a premium savings for you.

Finally, what about **mopeds**? They are operated on the street, but aren't subject to motor vehicle registration everywhere. Their slow speed can hinder traffic, yet they can be used to weave in and out of traffic. If a moped is not subject to registration, you would have liability coverage on premises under a homeowners policy, but no coverage off premises. (If it is subject to registration, homeowners liability coverage is not available.) A broader liability coverage is available under the miscellaneous type vehicle endorsement, which could be added to a PAP to provide coverage for mopeds—on premises and off premises.

Many insurers are not willing to provide coverage for mopeds, especially if there are underage operators. As a result, the specialty carrier market is often the only place to find coverage for mopeds.

A homeowners policy may be used to provide liability coverage for a **golf cart** which is used only on a golf course. If used on public streets or other areas, or if golf carts are subject to motor vehicle registration in the area where it is being used, an insured would need to obtain coverage under a miscellaneous type vehicle endorsement attached to a PAP or a specialty policy.

MOBILE HOMES

Over the last decade or so, the residential property insurance market has seen an increase in popularity in the purchase of mobile homes. At one time, just the words "mobile home" had the stigma of a cheaply constructed travel trailer that would burn up in an instant if it caught fire. As a result, it was difficult to insure them. But, the mobile home industry has come a long way, and mobile homeowners can now find coverage under ISO forms and a number of insurers now provide coverage under independently filed policy forms.

If you own or live in a mobile home, chances are you face most of the same property and liability exposures as does the owner of a traditionally built home. Hence, a homeowners policy is a sufficient base which, when endorsed to cover a mobile home, meets the general coverage needs of the mobile home owner.

A number of insurers participate in the mobile home coverage market by means of independently filed policy forms designed to address the special coverage needs of mobile home owners. Most of the same coverages provided by the ISO homeowners policy, as modified by attachment of a mobile home endorsement and related endorsements, are present in these policies. Specialty insurers also make available some independently filed endorsements providing different coverages and policy provisions than are available with an ISO policy. Some of these endorsements include:

- Variations of a number of traditional ISO endorsements, such as scheduled personal property coverage, earthquake coverage, additional living expense increased limits, personal property replacement cost coverage and loss assessment coverage.

- Endorsements unique to specialty mobile home insurers in general, or particular to one insurer, such as special coverage for outside antennas (including satellite dishes), and stated-value loss settlement (a valued policy approach).

- Endorsements allowing for seasonal occupancy or for vacancy.

- Variations of full repair or replacement cost valuation in the event of total or partial loss.

- Endorsements providing flood coverage (this is not National Flood Insurance Coverage, but coverage provided directly by the insurer).

Much of the risk evaluation performed regarding your mobile home, concerns the physical damage exposure of the structure itself. Age is a significant factor considered by underwriters—older mobile homes were not built with the same quality of construction standards that are in place today.

The weight and location of a mobile home are also considered for exposure to risk, as well as, the fact that a mobile home is "mobile" and exposed to increased risk of theft losses, or transportation perils.

WATERCRAFT INSURANCE

Recreational vehicles give us the motorized fun without the constraints of roads (along with the consequent hazards). Watercraft exposes an entirely new element, with no boundaries on operation (other than the shorelines) and little in the way of regulatory constraints on operation.

> **Watercraft range from small outboard flatboats used for fishing, to large outboard or inboard/outboard craft designed for several passengers and/or ski-behind capability. The term watercraft also includes the rapidly growing ranks of jet skis, large cabin cruisers and yachts.**

It's smart to inform your insurance agent if you buy a boat because an unendorsed homeowners policy provides very little in the way of coverage for your watercraft, either from a physical damage or a liability standpoint.

A homeowners policy limits personal property coverage for watercraft, including their trailers, furnishings, equipment and motors to only $1,000. Not only is this a relatively small dollar amount, the coverage is also subject to the applicable "perils insured against" named in the homeowners policy (and this would never include "perils of the seas" such as wave action, stranding, sinking or capsizing).

> **Under the windstorm and hail perils, a homeowners policy will only cover your watercraft and related equipment when it is inside a fully enclosed building. Since many boat owners store their boats outside (for example, on a trailer parked behind the garage), this eliminates coverage for an exposure to which the boat would be very susceptible to damage.**

Additionally, **theft coverage** for your watercraft is severely restricted under your homeowners policy. It applies only to theft that occurs on the residence premises. So, there would be no theft coverage if your boat and/or its trailer were stolen from a lakeside vacation location, from a parking lot in Yellowstone, or anywhere else away from the insured premises.

Boatowners face some of the same exposures to loss as do auto operators regarding the ownership, maintenance or use of watercraft, including:

- **Bodily injury and property damage** to others, such as injury to passengers, skiers, swimmers, occupants of other craft, damage to other craft, etc.

- **Physical damage** to the craft itself because of a number of perils such as collision with other boats or objects, fire and theft, "perils of the seas," including wave action, stranding, sinking or capsizing).

- **Injury** to the boat operator and other guests onboard the craft due to the actions of another boater who is uninsured.

- **Liability** imposed because of a responsibility for removing a wrecked craft from the waterway.

Whether a boat is eligible for homeowners liability coverage depends upon the ownership, use, power and length characteristics that apply to the boat and the particular situation.

So, while some liability coverage is provided, it is limited. If you own or use a boat that exceeds the power or length limitations you will have to look elsewhere for liability coverage. And even if you own a small boat which falls within the permitted range for liability coverage, you're likely to be motivated to look elsewhere for coverage, due to limitations on property coverage.

Remember: The maximum amount of personal property coverage for any kind of watercraft—including all related motors, equipment and trailers—under a homeowners policy is still $1,000. In many cases, this would represent only a small fraction of your actual exposure to a loss.

SPECIALIZED WATERCRAFT POLICIES

A **personal watercraft policy** is an independently filed specialty policy. The benefit of such a policy is that instead of trying to adapt an existing policy to meet only some of your needs, your insurer can craft a policy to meet your special needs. Generally, this includes physical damage coverage on an agreed-value or replacement-cost basis (instead of ACV), coverage for all risks of loss (instead of a limited package of perils), broader liability coverage, fewer restrictions on the types of eligible vessels, and coverage for injuries caused by uninsured boaters.

However, a personal watercraft policy doesn't include everything. The policy will not provide coverage for loss resulting from any of the following:

- Wear and tear, gradual deterioration, weathering, insects, mold, animal or marine life;

- Marring, scratching or denting;

- Osmosis, blistering or electrolysis (chemical and electrical reactions that take place in the fresh or salt water, and the gradual process is not the type of sudden and accidental damage intended to be covered by the policy);

- Manufacturer's defects or defects in design (Watercraft policies vary on this point, and some do provide coverage for defects in hull or machinery.);

- The cost of repairing or replacing any item having a "latent defect." (However, if such a flaw in material causes other damage, as in the case where a defective steering mechanism malfunctions and causes a collision, the policy will cover the resulting damage.)

Typically, these policies have coverage for equipment on shore, repairs, replacement for a prescribed list of property items, salvage charges, and commercial towing and assistance.

WATERCRAFT LIABILITY

The policy also provides coverage for five types of liability. Two of these are the typical bodily injury and property damage coverages found in other policies. The three additional coverages are somewhat particular to larger craft:

- attempted or actual raising, removal or destruction of the wreck of your insured property;

- failure to raise, remove, or destroy the wreck of your insured property; and

- liability to paid crew members under the Jones Act or other maritime law.

As mentioned earlier, this policy will also cover defense costs in addition to the limits of liability for losses.

Coverage not provided by a watercraft liability policy includes:

- liability of other covered persons to the named insured (such as the insured's spouse, or other residents of the insured's household);

- the named insured's liability to his or her own spouse or to any other person residing in the insured's household;

- liability assumed by the insured under contract or agreement;

- liability which arises while the insured's craft is being conveyed (towed) except at the point where the boat is hauled out of the water or launched;

- fines or other penalties which any government unit requires the insured to pay;

and

- punitive damages.

You may want to purchase **yacht trailer coverage**, which provides physical damage coverage for specified trailers used exclusively for transporting your vessel. A similar provision is found in most personal watercraft policies.

Coverage is provided on the basis of all risks of direct loss coverage, subject to a few exclusions (wear and tear, gradual deterioration and manufacturer's defects). In contrast, usually personal watercraft policies limit physical damage coverage for trailers to a list of named perils.

PERSONAL PROPERTY COVERAGE WHILE ON BOARD

This insurance provides coverage for personal property of you and your family members while on board the vessel or being loaded or unloaded. This applies to such things as clothing, personal effects, fishing gear and sports equipment (there is no coverage for money, jewelry, travelers checks, or valuable papers and documents).

Most personal watercraft policies for smaller craft do not provide this type of coverage.

If you have a yacht. You may want to check out different yacht policies. Ask your insurer what types of policies are offered. They generally tend to have different coverages and a different set of exclusions.

CONCLUSION

If you are looking for broad coverage on an all-risk basis and your homeowners policy does not offer full coverage for your personal possessions because they don't fit the average risk scenario, you may want to purchase a specialty policy.

This chapter has mentioned just a few specialty policies that insurers offer. If you are interested in specialty insurance for a specific item, you may want to talk to your agent or insurer. Chapter 9 will discuss how to value your personal possessions, and also will help you determine how much insurance you need.

CHAPTER 9

VALUING YOUR THINGS AND BUYING ENOUGH COVERAGE

Once you have determined what you want to insure, your next step is to determine what value your possessions have and how much coverage you need to buy.

A number of factors will go into your purchase of coverage. But, your choice of which coverage to purchase will probably be influenced by some of the following questions:

- What coverage, if any do you have currently?

- What type of coverage do you need or want?

- Do you have a lot of valuables?

- How are the possessions used?

- How much will optional coverage cost (the more coverage being purchased, the higher the premium)?

First things first. Do you know how much coverage you have?

Chances are, you don't even think about how much you have until your premium bill arrives. Or until it comes time to file a claim.

> For most people, the topic of how much coverage they have, doesn't come up until a tree crashes through their living room, a fire barbecues their kitchen, or a burglar makes off with the family silver.

The problem is, until you file a claim, you probably won't know whether or not your insurance company will provide a fair and fast settlement. Many factors can cause problems with a policy or a claim.

When shopping for insurance, it's a good idea to anticipate these problems as fully as possible—and avoid them.

This is why it is important to properly value your possessions and make sure that you purchase enough coverage.

> Most disputes between insurance companies and policy owners center on coverage issues—whether or not a particular loss is insured by a policy. The main mechanism insurance companies use to protect themselves against the negative finan-

> cial impact of big claims is to deny coverage on
> some fundamental issue with no relation to the
> specifics of the claim.

Understanding the concepts behind these problems is an essential tool to finding the right insurance solution for you and your possessions. This chapter will discuss how to value your things and buy enough coverage for a loss.

VALUING YOUR STUFF

Often, a loss occurs and people find themselves stuck in the impossible position of trying to remember everything they own. What was in my jewelry box? What pictures were hanging in the living room? How many CDs did I have? You can prevent having to play this memory game by valuing your things ahead of time (preferably at the time of purchase).

One simple way to do this is to make a list of everything you own that is part of your household. This includes furniture (including carpets, drapes, etc.), art or other decorations, appliances, clothes and other possessions. To organize the list, you can simply divide the list into relevant rooms in the house. (For guidance refer to the chart back in Chapter 1.)

> Assigned values work best if you remember to
> save receipts or bills. You should also keep other
> support documents— including any photos you

> **have or serial numbers from large appliances and electronic equipment.**

COVERAGE TERMS

Look close at the coverage terms of a homeowners or renters policy, there are several options you may choose from and different policies may apply a variety of the **loss settlement terms** to different kinds of property. In other words, your policy may provide **full replacement value** for a sofa, but only offer **actual cash value** for your dining room table.

An **actual cash value policy** pays the amount needed to replace the item, minus depreciation. If, for instance, a fire destroyed the oak dining table that you paid $1000 for five years ago, you would only receive $750 for it, assuming it had a 10-year life and would cost $1,500 to replace at today's prices.

A **replacement cost policy** would pay you the full $1,500. For most people, this type of coverage is worth the extra 10 to 15 percent that insurance companies typically charge for it.

> **Insurers often use the term "full replacement value" freely, even though the term applies in relatively few policies. So, be sure to determine ahead of time which of these loss settlement terms applies to your policy.**

A particularly high valued item may be insured by a **floater**. Floaters are written as separate polices or as endorsements to standard policies. For more information on floaters turn to Chapter 5 of this book.

You can also buy additional **blanket coverage** for a specific category of protection. Instead of buying an expensive floater for your grandfather's wristwatch, you may want to raise your coverage in the jewelry category from the $1,000 limit to a $5,000 limit.

Be careful: most insurers limit the amount you can collect for any single item under a blanket policy. The limit for most companies tends to vary enormously— sometimes between $500 and $5,000.

REVIEW COVERAGE EVERY FEW YEARS

One of the most important things to consider regarding insurance is not to assume that everything has been taken care of—or that it has been taken care of in the best way to fit your needs.

If you rely on your insurance company or agent to set your policy limits and to keep those limits updated, you may find yourself **underinsured** when you file a claim. This can be a serious problem. In extreme situations, you can deal with underinsurance by having your policy upgraded retroactively. But this kind of solution is rare—and getting rarer, as insurance companies operate on ever-thinner reserves and profit margins.

An important point to remember when buying insurance: All types of coverage pose certain exclusions. Some people overlook these exceptions when reading through their policy and later find out that their assets were not protected under their policy.

It is important to know when coverage does and does not apply. You should know the common restrictions of your policy before you purchase it.

INSURING AGAINST THEFT

When you are insuring possessions it is particularly important to account for your **theft prone items**.

The following is a list of only a few items that have a high-risk for theft:

antiques	electronic equipment
art objects	photography equipment
figurines	power tools
calculators	furs
silver	clock radios
guns	sports equipment
clocks	jewelry
stereos	collections
lawn mowers	televisions
computers	musical instruments
typewriters	electrical appliances
vacuum cleaners	

According to the National Crime Prevention Council (NCPC), property crimes are the most frequently reported crimes in this country. Experts estimate that 99 percent of us will be a victim of theft at least once in our lifetimes.

Whether you own something of little value or materials costing hundreds of thousands of dollars, you can still experience a theft. About three out of ten losses involve less than $50; about one in ten involves a loss of $1,000 or more, said the NCPC.

> **The larger your home, the greater your risk of theft. If there are six or more members in your household, you would be three times more likely to experience a theft than a household with just one member.**

After you have conducted an inventory of everything you own, your insurance agent will help you determine the value of your possessions. This will give you an idea of how much coverage you will need to purchase.

If you don't want to use an agent, ask your insurer if they can provide you with **historical price ranges** for the various kinds of personal property that you are insuring.

> Your high-valued possessions may not be fully insurable under your homeowners policy. These policies usually have limits on high-priced items like jewelry or expensive electronics. If you own these things, you may want to check out the other coverages discussed in this book.

THEFT COVERAGE ENDORSEMENTS

> People often assume they have theft coverage when they don't.

If you purchased dwelling property coverage to save some money, you probably don't have any **theft coverage** for your personal property. In some cases, even broad homeowners policies don't offer theft coverage that's broad enough or deep enough to satisfy your specific needs. However, in either case, theft coverage may be added to an insurance policy by endorsement.

There are two variations of theft coverage—the **broad theft coverage** endorsement which is available for owner occupants of a dwelling, and the **limited theft coverage** endorsement which is available for renters and other non-owner occupants.

Limited theft coverage, when repackaged slightly and sold as stand-alone insurance, is sometimes called **renters insurance**.

Broad theft coverage applies to more types of property, offers optional off-premises coverage, and insures other members of the insured's family who are members of the same household. Limited theft coverage applies only on the insured premises, and doesn't provide any coverage for your family.

Since the primary focus of this book is to insure your personal possessions at any location, we will focus on broad theft coverage.

PERILS INSURED AGAINST

Under a broad theft coverage endorsement you are insured against losses by only two perils—theft, including attempted theft, and vandalism or malicious mischief as a result of theft or attempted theft.

A caveat: No coverage for vandalism or malicious mischief is offered when the dwelling has been vacant for more than 30 days immediately before a loss. The reason: vacant buildings are often at high risk for vandalism losses, because a thief or vandal has a low expectation of being caught.

Defining the word "vacant" can cause some disputes between you and your insurance company.

But, generally, it means the dwelling has no occupants or furnishings. (A furnished dwelling is simply "unoccupied," not vacant.)

COVERAGE AND LIMITS

If a theft occurs on your property, a limit of liability may apply to your coverage for the incident. Generally, insurers will pay for any one covered loss at the **described location**.

Limits for on-premises coverage must be shown in the Declarations.

On-premises coverage applies to property owned or used by you, and to property owned by a residence employee. It also applies away from the described location if property has been placed for safekeeping in one of the places described. (But property would not be covered while in transit, or at any other locations.)

Off-premises coverage is not required, but it is only available when on-premises coverage is purchased.

When this type of coverage is purchased, a separate limit must be shown in addition to the limit for on-premises coverage. This endorsement does not cover loss to personal property away from the described location caused by theft or vandalism or malicious mischief unless a limit is shown for on-premises coverage. Coverage applies while property is away from the described location if property is owned or used by you, or owned by a "residence employee" while in a dwelling occupied by you or while working for you.

This coverage applies away from the described location, but not to property at a newly acquired **princi-**

pal residence. (A "principal residence" would qualify for on-premises coverage.)

If you move, you will have up to 30 days at a newly acquired principal residence to contact your insurer. This coverage is broader than purely "on-premises" coverage, because it applies at each location and while property is in transit between them.

Coverage will only apply at the new location as soon as moving is complete.

SPECIAL LIMITS OF LIABILITY

These limits do not increase the limit of liability applicable to **on-premises** coverage or **off-premises** coverage. The special limit for each numbered category is the total limit for each loss for all property in that category.

- $200 on money, bank notes, bullion, gold other than goldware, silver other than silverware, platinum, coins and medals.

- $1,000 on securities, accounts, deeds, evidences of debt, letters of credit, notes other than bank notes, manuscripts, passports, personal records, tickets and stamps.

- $1,000 on watercraft, including their trailers, furnishings, equipment and outboard motors.

- $1,000 on trailers not used with watercraft.

- $1,000 on grave markers.

- $1,000 on jewelry, watches, furs, precious and semiprecious stones.

- $2,000 on firearms.

- $2,500 on silverware, goldware, gold-placed ware and pewterware. (This includes flatware, hollowware, tea sets, trays and trophies made of or including silver, gold or pewter.)

These limits are sublimits that apply to certain kinds of property. Similar limits are found on homeowners policies.

The intent is to provide some basic coverage for these special items of value which may be the subject of theft losses. However, some individuals collect particular items and may have disproportionate exposures which are not contemplated in average insurance rates. If you have large exposures, higher limits may be available for an additional premium charge.

Or you may want to look into a separate personal property floater, which insures specific pieces of property against theft or damage.

There is no coverage for animals, birds or fish, and property of tenants or boarders who are not related to you.

Your pets may not be covered under a theft policy, but some companies do write these types of policies. Shop

around you'd be surprised at the number of companies offering not only medical expense coverage for
your pet, but also coverage for theft, strays, and even
liability. For more information on pet coverage, turn
to Chapter 8.

Coverage applies at other locations you temporarily
occupied, but not a location owned or rented by you
which is not the described location.

Sometimes insurance companies will require other
kinds of location conditions. In the 1994 decision *Sirius
Insurance Co. et al. v. Paul Collins*, the United States
Court of Appeals in New York considered the theft of
a pleasure boat while it was stored ashore.

Sirius issued a one-year policy under its High Performance Marine Program to Collins covering his vessel, a Midnight Express 37 Sport, and its trailer.

The policy included a "theft warranty" relating to
periods of out-of-water storage that conditioned coverage upon certain precautions to be taken by the insured, as well as on the theft occurring in specified
fashion. The provision read:

> It is hereby understood and agreed and war-
> ranted that, while the insured boat is stored
> on a trailer it shall be:
>
> 1. Kept in locked fences [sic] enclosure, ga-
> rage or building.
>
> 2. Secured with a trailer ball lock while at-
> tached to a vehicle.
>
> It is understood and agreed that this certifi-
> cate does not cover loss or damage caused

by theft of the insured boat(s), and/or equipment, while stored on the trailer unless occasioned by person or persons making:

1. illegal entry to the locked fenced enclosure, garage or building; or

2. destruction of the ball lock.

Provided that the above is accompanied by actual force and violence of which there shall be visible marks made by tools, explosives, electricity or chemicals.

On or around January 5, 1992, Collins removed the boat from the water for winter storage, loaded it onto the insured trailer, and towed it to his parents' home in West Islip, New York. He parked his truck and the trailered boat, attached with a ball lock, in the circular driveway at the front of his parents' home.

He planned to leave it there "for an indefinite period of time."

The following day the truck, trailer and boat were missing from the driveway.

Sirius declined Collins's claim, arguing that the theft warranty required him to place the boat, while stored on a trailer, in a locked and fenced enclosure. When he failed to lock it up, he breached the terms of the warranty.

Collins sued. The district court ruled for Sirius. Collins appealed, making two arguments.

First, he contended that, because the theft occurred ashore, litigation under the policy is not within the specialized exclusive maritime jurisdiction conferred on federal courts.

The appeals court rejected this argument. It ruled that a policy of marine insurance, which covered a vessel against perils while afloat and during transportation or storage ashore, served "the protection of maritime commerce." Even though the policy included coverage during land storage and that the theft occurred in those circumstances, it still fell under maritime jurisdiction.

Second, Collins's contended that the theft warranty was ambiguous and had to be construed against Sirius. He argued the ambiguity was created because the lack of a conjunctive "and" or "or" left it unclear whether he was required to comply with one or both of the listed precautions against theft (specifically, storage in a locked fenced enclosure and securing with a trailer ball lock while attached to a vehicle).

The appeals court didn't agree with this argument, either. "The [warranty] naturally and unambiguously conveys that both precautionary conditions must be met," it wrote. "As to the content, although the contract is poorly drafted and contains odd provisions of questionable value on either reading, we do not find that inferring a disjunctive makes better sense than the apparently implied [meaning] and we therefore do not find ambiguity that would require construing the contract against the insurer."

It supported Sirius's rejection of the claim because property in the custody of a laundry, cleaner or similar service operation is covered only for loss by burglary or robbery (there is no coverage if property simply disappears, or is taken by employees). This type of coverage can be purchased by the establishment— it covers the bailee for any damage to or theft of your property while on the premises. Property in the mail is not covered.

CONDITIONS

A broad theft coverage endorsement has only two conditions which, in effect, modify conditions found on the dwelling property coverage form to which it is attached. (Broad theft coverage is usually an endorsement to a dwelling policy.)

The first condition adds a requirement that you notify the police when a theft loss occurs. This is a common condition on policies that include theft coverage. Since an unendorsed dwelling policy does not include theft coverage, it does not include this condition.

The next condition modifies the "other insurance" condition so that theft coverage will apply proportionally based on limits when a loss is covered by this endorsement and other insurance. For other types of losses, the other insurance clause found in the dwelling property form will still apply.

If a loss covered by this endorsement is also covered by other insurance, the insurer will pay only the proportion of the loss that the limit of liability that applies under this endorsement bears to the total amount of insurance covering the loss.

An example of how the other insurance condition

works: You have $10,000 of on-premises theft coverage under a broad theft endorsement and a separate policy that covers personal property theft losses for up to $15,000 ($25,000 of total coverage). If a $5,000 loss occurs, only $2,000 of the loss is covered by this endorsement.

CONCLUSION

Of course, insurance consumers—like consumers of anything—should compare the various products they're considering buying. Read the policies closely when determining what insurance to purchase

It is important to compare and contrast policies in order to find the coverage that individually suits you and obtain that coverage at premiums that you can afford.

It is important to compare not only insurance companies but the prices and limits within each insurance company as well. If you follow the guidelines provided throughout this book, with some shopping around and just a few adjustments you will be able to find coverage in a package that suits you and your needs. This chapter reviewed some basic buying guidelines and tips that smart insurance consumers can follow to maintain cost-effective coverage on their personal possessions.

Chapter 10 will discuss some important definitions that apply to insuring your possessions.

CHAPTER 10

KEY
DEFINITIONS

Before you can file a claim and find coverage you must first understand the language of your policy. And because each line of insurance interprets its policies and definitions differently, it is important to understand how the language and basic concepts pertain to your specific policy.

This is true whether it is a policy for your car, home, life or your personal possessions. This chapter will detail the basic terms which will affect the coverage of your possessions.

BLANKET COVERAGE

Blanket coverage provides a single amount of insurance that may apply to different types of property or to different locations. The word "blanket" comes from the fact that a single limit of insurance applies.

There are three ways to write a blanket limit: a single limit may apply to all types of property at a specific location, a single limit may apply to one type of property at multiple locations (i.e., a blanket amount for "buildings" only), or a single limit may apply to all types of property at multiple locations. One advantage of blanket coverage is that it allows you to move property (such as supplies or merchandise) between locations without having to worry about adjusting the limits of insurance at each location.

BROAD THEFT COVERAGE

Dwelling forms do not provide any theft coverage for personal property. The **broad theft coverage** endorsement may be added to a dwelling policy to provide coverage for the **owner occupant** of the dwelling. For an additional premium, the endorsement covers personal property owned or used by you, or owned by a residence employee, against direct physical loss from the perils insured against.

CANCELLATION

You may cancel a policy at any time and for any reason. You simply have to notify the company in writing.

However, the company may cancel a policy only at certain times and for certain reasons. In addition, you must send a notice of cancellation to your insurer a prescribed number of days before it becomes effective.

CLAIM EXPENSE

Claim expense coverage includes the costs of defending a claim, court costs charged against an insured in any suit the insurer defends, and premiums on bonds which do not exceed the coverage limit and which are required in a suit defended by the insurer. When the insurer requests the assistance of an insured in investigating or defending a claim, reasonable expenses of the insured, including loss of earnings up to $50 per day, are covered. Claim expense insurance also covers post-judgment interest which accrues prior to actual payment.

CONCURRENT CAUSATION

Concurrent causation is a term that refers to a situation where two or more perils act concurrently (at the same time or in sequence) to cause a loss. This can create significant problems for insurers when one of the perils is covered by a policy and the other peril is not.

DATE OF LOSS

This provision states that, for the purpose of the coverages, the date on which the insurer receives written notice that the lienholder has complied with all of the recovery conditions shall be treated as the **date of loss**.

DWELLING PROPERTY COVERAGE

Dwelling property coverage includes coverage for your dwelling, other structures on the grounds, personal property owned by your family members, and certain types of loss of use, such as rental value or additional living expenses. The terms "dwelling insurance" and "fire insurance" are often used interchangeably.

You might consider buying a separate dwelling policy if you don't need the full package of homeowners coverages. For example: If you own two houses, you can extend your homeowners policy to cover liability risks for additional premises, in which case you'd only need dwelling property coverage at the second residence. This usually ends up being less expensive than buying two complete homeowners packages.

FALLING OBJECTS

This peril does not include loss to property contained in the building unless the roof or an outside wall of the building is first damaged by a falling object.

> **Damage to the falling object itself is not covered.**

Falling objects can be anything from a meteorite to a part of an airplane. But it has to penetrate the outer wall or roof of your house before the personal possessions damaged inside are covered.

FIRE

Fire is not defined in the policy, but the policy intends to cover fire losses accompanied by flame. A smoldering cigarette on a sofa is not a "fire" until it breaks into flame. Also the fire must be "hostile," that is, out of its natural environment. Heat damage done to a wall near a wood heating stove would not be covered. If a spark from a fireplace shot out and caught the drapes on fire, there would be coverage.

In order for smoke damage to be covered, it must be sudden and accidental. An example: You leave a roast unattended in the oven while you run a quick errand. Upon returning, you find that a small fire has broken out in the oven and heavy smoke has damaged draperies and upholstered dining room chairs. The expensive cleaning and smoke removal would be covered.

GENERAL EXCLUSIONS

General exclusions are broad in scope and deal with perils which affect a large number of households at the same time. Perils such as earthquakes, floods, nuclear incidents and war are some of the principal general exclusions.

Whether the loss is caused directly or indirectly by these excluded perils, there is no coverage.

Also, if losses resulting from the perils excluded by the general exclusions occur with perils covered under the policy, either at the same time or in a prior or later sequence, there will be no coverage. An example: Due to an earthquake, several pipes are broken and water damages walls, floors and personal property. Normally, the water damage is covered, but because it occurred in connection with an earthquake, no coverage applies.

HOMEOWNERS POLICY

A **homeowners policy** is a complete package of property and liability coverages designed to cover the average residential and personal exposures of most individuals and families.

A policy may be issued to cover a premises used principally for private residential purposes (some incidental business occupancies, such as a studio or office, are permitted), and which contains no more than two family living units (single family homes and duplexes are eligible). Separate policies are also available for tenants of apartment buildings and condominium unit owners, who only have personal property and liability exposures and do not need to insure the dwelling.

A point to remember: Homeowners insurance covers the value of the home or homes in which you live—not just the physical property. In other words, the insurance should cover risks and liabilities that might encumber the value of your property.

INDEMNIFICATION

Indemnification for a loss may be payment in money or replacement of the property. Stolen property may be returned to the insured, and payment made for any damage, or the company may keep the property and pay the insured an agreed or appraised amount.

INLAND MARINE

The term **inland marine** insurance as it relates to personal coverage encompasses property which has special coverage needs for one or both of the following reasons: it is mobile; and its value is intrinsic or market-driven.

INSURED LOCATION

Insured location is a sweeping definition which frequently applies to liability coverages. It is identical on all forms, and includes all of the following:

- the residence premises;

- any other premises used by the insured as a residence and identified in the Declarations or acquired during the policy period;

- any premises used in connection with the residence premises or a newly-acquired premises;

- any non-owned premises where an insured temporarily resides;

- vacant land owned by or rented to an insured (but not farm land);

- land owned by or rented to an insured on which a one- or two-family dwelling is being constructed as a residence for any insured;

- individual or family cemetery plots or burial vaults of any insured; and

- any part of a premises rented to any insured for non-business purposes.

INSURED (NAMED)

"You" and "your" refer to the "named insured" shown in the Declarations and the spouse if a resident of the same household. "We," "us" and "our" refer to the company providing this insurance.

A named insured is different from an insured or an insurable interest under the policy. A named insured is the person whose name appears on the front of the policy—and the spouse, whether named on the front page or not, as long as he or she lives in the same household. (More than one named insured can appear on the front page.)

An insured could be a relative residing with the named insured or a guest of the named insured.

In legal disputes, courts will sometimes include any entity with an insurable interest in a dwelling as an insured, too. For example: A bank or other financial institution may have an insurable interest in your property by virtue of a mortgage. It might then be an insured under your policy.

INSURING AGREEMENT

The **insuring agreement** states that the **policy term** begins (inception date) and ends (expiration date) at 12:01 A.M. standard time at the location of the property involved. In some states, the policies are written to begin and end at noon. In either case, pinpointing the time to an exact minute and location is more specific than the term stated in the Declarations.

The insuring agreement also includes an **assignment clause**, which supports the concept of a personal contract. If the property is sold, the policy may not be assigned to the new owner "except with the written consent of the Company." This gives the insurer the opportunity to reevaluate the risk under the new ownership before agreeing to any assignment.

LIABILITY INSURANCE

Liability insurance is known as "third party" coverage, because it pays damages suffered by others when you are responsible. Injuries suffered by you or your family members are not covered.

Acts of an insured while serving as an officer of a corporation or member of a board of directors are generally excluded because this is a **professional liability exposure**. But coverage is provided if the insured is acting for a nonprofit organization and receives no pay for services.

LIABILITY LIMIT

The **liability limit** on the policy is the maximum amount which will be paid for any one occurrence. An occurrence is defined as an accident or an exposure to substantially the same conditions over a period of time which causes an injury. The policy limit of liability is not increased because there is more than one insured person, nor is it increased because there is more than one claim or claimant as a result of a single occurrence.

LIGHTNING

Lightning is a peril which is usually thought of as

damaging to real property; however, if a lightning bolt hits a dwelling's electrical system, it can damage television sets, computer equipment or other electronic equipment. This type of damage is covered even if there is no ensuing fire.

LOSS (TYPES OF LOSS)

Many of the major coverages, such as coverage for buildings and contents, provide insurance for direct losses. **Direct loss** means actual physical damage, destruction or loss of property. Fire damage and stolen merchandise are examples of direct physical damage or loss.

Other coverages provide insurance for **indirect losses**, which also are known as **consequential losses**. Indirect losses are those that result from direct losses, and occur as a consequence of direct loss. If fire destroys an office building, the loss of the building is a direct loss.

However, the business is likely to experience other losses because of the loss of the building. There may be a period of business interruption, during which business income is lost because operations have stopped.

Intentional Loss is the subject of many arguments between insurance companies and insureds.

This exclusion makes it clear that the policy is not designed to cover damage caused intentionally by the insured. To do so would create a **moral hazard**.

OCCURRENCE

An **occurrence** is usually defined as an accident, or an exposure to substantially the same conditions over a period of time, which causes damage or injury. For example, water leaking from your outside pipes softens the ground under your neighbor's garage, eventually causing its partial collapse. This would be considered a single "occurrence."

Pay attention to the way in which "occurrence" is defined in any policy you sign. Insurance companies that don't want to pay homeowners claims will sometimes make tortuous arguments that whatever went wrong doesn't qualify as an occurrence.

PERILS (CAUSES OF LOSS)

> **Most property insurance policies insure against perils rather than hazards.**

Property policies usually insure against loss or damage caused by perils. Fire, lightning, explosion, windstorm, vandalism and theft are perils. Homeowners policies include a section called "Perils Insured Against." By definition, perils are "causes of loss."

PERILS (NAMED VS. ALL RISK)

Property insurance policies are often written on a **specified peril** basis (also called "**named perils**").

Such policies specifically identify the perils insured against.

A number of insurers in this country started out as "fire insurance" companies, and originally fire insurance was the only coverage they wrote. In its purest form, fire insurance would only cover direct loss or damage caused by fire. Over time, the fire insurance field evolved into a broader property insurance field. Fire insurance policies began covering losses caused by fire and lightning. Eventually, wind and hail coverage became widely available. Options for adding coverage for additional perils grew until there were standardized groupings of insurable perils—"extended coverage" or "EC" meant a package of seven-to-nine specific perils, and "broad form" coverage included all the EC perils plus six-to-ten others. Policies which name many perils are known as **multi-peril** policies. Most property insurance today is written on multi-peril forms. Multi-peril policies are still "named peril" policies.

There were logical reasons for linking multiple perils in the same insurance policy. When an explosion or lightning bolt damages a building and causes a fire, it is often difficult to attribute portions of the loss to each separate peril, and settling the loss would be a problem if only the fire loss is insured. When all contributing perils are covered, a multiple peril policy eliminates the problem of having to determine how much of a given loss has been caused by each peril.

The broadest coverage of all is provided by **special forms**, which historically were known as "**all risk**" forms. An all-risk coverage form does not name insured perils — it covers all perils and risks of loss which are not specifically excluded. (For this reason, they are also known as "**open peril**" forms.) Although the coverage is very broad, a special coverage form always includes a long list of exclusions. The exclusions are necessary to limit the coverage to what the insurer intends to cover. The terms "special" and "all risk" coverage became synonymous because policies used to say they covered "all risks of physical loss *except... .*" In recent years the word "all" has been removed from the policy language, because "all-risk" policies never truly intended to cover "all risks of loss" and it was feared that insureds and courts would misinterpret the coverage. The policies now say they insure against "risks of direct loss" except for what is excluded. The change was made to clarify intent and to reduce misunderstanding.

You should remember that a "specified perils" form names the perils insured against, while a "special form" covers insured property against all risks of loss which are not excluded.

PERSONAL ARTICLES FLOATER

The **personal articles floater** (PAF) is a basic form used to insure certain classes of property on an itemized basis. It is virtually identical to the "Scheduled Personal Property Endorsement," which may be attached to a homeowners policy. These two forms illustrate the extent to which the distinction between lines of insurance has become blurred — the same coverage may be issued as a separate inland marine policy or as personal property insurance.

PERSONAL AUTO POLICY

The **personal auto policy** (PAP) is a simplified and more personalized contract than its predecessors. The personal auto policy contains only about half as many words as the family automobile policy did, but it provides essentially the same coverages. The shift from "family" to "personal" coverage has no bearing on the type of risk eligible for coverage — the PAP is designed to insure individuals and entire families. The title word "personal" serves only to distinguish the insurance from "business" coverage.

PERSONAL LINES INSURANCE

Dwelling and homeowner coverages are among those classified as **personal lines insurance**. These coverages may only be written for property which is used principally for private residential purposes, and the named insured is usually an individual or a married couple. Many dwellings in this country are insured by homeowner policies, but dwelling policies are still issued for a variety of reasons. Some dwellings are ineligible for homeowners coverage because of the building's age, location or value.

Other dwellings are ineligible because of the number of living units involved—a homeowners policy may be used to cover one- or two-unit residential property, while dwelling forms may cover a structure containing up to four living units. An owner of property having more than four living units must look to commercial forms for coverage. Dwelling policies are primarily issued to cover non-owner occupied buildings.

PERSONAL PROPERTY

Personal property includes all forms of property other than real property. On a homeowners policy, personal property coverage protects household goods, furniture, appliances and other personal belongings which may range from clothing and toys to home computers and small boats.

On commercial policies, personal property means business property such as merchandise, office furniture and supplies.

PROPERTY DAMAGE

Property damage means physical injury to, destruction of, or loss of use of tangible property.

Notice that "property damage" includes loss of use. If you damage your neighbor's home, your neighbor might have to live somewhere else while the home is being repaired or rebuilt. The extra expenses for loss of use (rent, meals, transportation) could be claimed in addition to the actual damages to the home.

REASONABLE EXPENSE

Be careful of the phrase **reasonable expense**. Some contractors will bid low to get insurance work, and then charge a lot for things like debris removal. Your insurer won't pay these fees if they're too high—25 percent over average for your area will alert some companies. If you use a contractor other than one recommended by your insurance company, make sure all bids include debris removal costs.

REMOVAL

Removal coverage means the coverage of property removed from the premises to protect it from a peril insured against. Coverage applies to direct loss from any cause while the property is removed. This coverage does not change the limit of insurance for the property removed.

RENTERS POLICY

A **renters policy** generally protects the possessions of tenants in a house or apartment against 17 named perils. It also provides liability coverage but doesn't protect the actual dwelling, which should be covered under the landlord's policy. Renters who don't want to pay for liability protection can opt for a policy that covers only personal property.

The policy for co-op and condominium owners provides coverage for liability and personal property, much like HO-4. While insurance purchased by the co-op or condominium association covers much of the actual dwelling, individual owners who want coverage for improvements to their units must write them into an HO-6 policy. If you add a porch, for instance, you'll need an endorsement (an addition to your policy that expands its coverage).

REPLACEMENT COST COVERAGE

Replacement cost coverage is available for commercial buildings and some contents, such as machinery and equipment. When the coverage applies, losses are settled on the basis of the actual replacement cost at the time of loss, without any deduction for depreciation.

Most policies will pay replacement cost only if the property is actually repaired or replaced — if it is not, the loss will be paid on an ACV basis. For buildings, policies typically require that you maintain a minimum amount of insurance (usually 80 percent of the current replacement cost value) in order for replacement cost coverage to apply.

REPORTING FORMS

Another variation affecting insurance limits is the use of **reporting forms** which allow the amount of insurance to fluctuate during the policy period. When a business has changing inventory values during the year, a fixed amount of insurance would be inappropriate — at times the business might be "overinsured" and at other times "underinsured." Reporting forms were created to avoid the costly situation of overinsurance, problems with underinsurance, and the inconvenience of having to continually endorse policies to change limits.

Full reporting is required. If values are underreported, the insurer will not pay a greater proportion of a loss than the amount reported divided by the actual value. For example, if the actual value is $60,000 and the insured reports $40,000, only two-thirds of any loss would be covered by the insurance. The full reporting requirement is also known as the "honesty clause," because the penalty for underreporting takes away any incentive to underreport values in the hope of paying a lower insurance premium.

RESIDENCE PREMISES

Residence premises means the dwelling, other structures and grounds, or that part of any other building where the named insured lives, and which is identified as the residence premises in the Declarations.

RISK

Risk is the uncertainty about loss, and transferring risk is the most important function of insurance. "Peril" is a cause of loss, or a potential cause of loss. "Hazard" is something that increases the likelihood that a loss will occur because of a peril, or something that is likely to increase the extent of a loss in the event that a loss does occur. While fire is a peril, such things as frayed electrical wires and containers of flammable liquids are hazards.

SCHEDULING COVERAGE

Schedule coverage may be used to provide different amounts of insurance for different types of property at one or more locations. It is a variation of specific insurance, because each item on the schedule is "specific." Schedule coverage might be used when you have multiple buildings and multiple types of personal property to insure. A schedule is used to itemize the types and locations of property and the limits of insurance that apply to each.

SEVERABILITY

Severability of insurance means that each insured person as defined in the policy has the same rights and obligations that would exist had a separate policy been issued to each. However, this severability does not increase the limits of liability under the policy.

SPECIFIC COVERAGE

Specific coverage provides a specific amount of insurance for specific types of property at specific locations. An example would be a form providing a limit of insurance of $100,000 for a building and $50,000 for personal property at a single location.

SUBROGATION

Simply explained, **subrogation** means that, once the insurance company has paid you for the loss you sustained, it has all the rights in or to that claim. An example: Your neighbor loses control of his car and crashes into your garage, causing considerable damage. Your insurance company, after paying you, has the right to sue your neighbor for the damages he caused. However, if before any loss occurs you waive in writing all rights of recovery against any person, then the company no longer has the right of subrogation. If you don't do this, and if the company does subrogate a loss, you must sign and deliver to the company all necessary papers and cooperate with them in any reasonable way they might request to collect from the party responsible for the loss.

TERRITORIAL LIMITS

Typical of the broad coverage provided by personal inland marine coverage forms, the scheduled personal property endorsement states that the **coverage terri-**

tory for most classes of property is worldwide. However, one qualifier applies to fine art—this class of property is covered only within the United States and Canada.

THEFT

The word **theft** is broadly defined as the wrongful taking of property and includes burglary, holdup or stealing. For example: You discover a television set missing from your home and no signs that the house has been burglarized. It would be presumed that this is a theft since the property could not have just been lost or misplaced.

The circumstances surrounding the loss of property must be such that there can be presumption of theft. There's no coverage for theft of materials or supplies to be used for construction of a dwelling.

> Theft by a member of your household is not covered nor is property stolen from a room you rent out. So, before you hand over the keys to your summer house to friends, check this part of your policy.

UMBRELLA COVERAGE

An **umbrella policy** is designed to provide liability insurance on an excess basis, above underlying primary insurance coverages or a self-insured retention. (This means a deductible for losses which are not covered by primary insurance.) Generally, the scope of the coverage is broad and the limits of coverage are high. Insurance companies usually require substantial amounts of underlying coverages (personal liability, automobile liability, etc.) for known exposures before they will issue an umbrella policy.

Underlying policy or "underlying insurance" means any policy providing the "insured" with initial or primary liability insurance covering one or more of the types of liability listed in the deductible section of the Declarations of a policy.

CONCLUSION

These are a few of the basic definitions that apply to insuring your personal possessions. These definitions and others occur throughout the book to provide you with the tools necessary to understand the language involved in insuring your valuables.

Chapter 11 will discuss the claims process.

KEY DEFINITIONS

CHAPTER 11

MAKING CLAIMS

All the effort you put into purchasing the right kind of insurance coverage comes into play when you have to **make a claim** on your policy.

As a policyholder, instead of sitting back and waiting for a disaster to happen, you should familiarize yourself with the steps that go into the claims-making process to avoid costly and time consuming mistakes.

According to the Insurance Information Institute, more than $75 billion are paid out each year to policyholders with claims resulting from losses suffered during fires, hurricanes, tornadoes, robberies, auto accidents, dog bites, falls and a host of other traumatic accidents.

It is important to remember that filing a claim is a process, and knowing you rights through this process can be pivotal to getting your claim paid.

Your insurance company at any time and for any reason has the right to investigate any claim that you make. But if you present your circumstances effectively, your insurance company may allow your claim, which can save you a crucial amount in expenses. This chapter will focus on the most effective way to make a claim and get it paid in the event of loss to your personal possessions.

The process of making a claim and getting it paid is the **adjustment process**. To make this process work for you, it is first important to know what your duties are when a loss occurs.

YOUR DUTIES AT THE TIME OF A LOSS

If you experience an insurable loss, there are several **duties required of you** as a policy owner before your coverage can kick in. If you don't follow these rules, you may wind up paying for the loss out of your own pocket, as did this couple in a 1989 case of misrepresentation in Missouri.

In January of 1981, Barbara and David Meeker purchased a homeowners policy from Shelter insurance to cover the Meekers' home and its contents.

In July of 1983, the Meeker home and all of its contents were destroyed by fire.

The Meekers filed a claim which Shelter denied, contending that the policy was void because the Meekers had made false representations regarding prior fire losses, when they applied for coverage. Shelter said it would not have issued the policy if it had known about these prior losses.

After the fire in question, which the evidence indicates was of incendiary origin, the Meekers were contacted by Robert Barnett, an adjuster for Shelter, who took recorded statements from them regarding the fire.

Mrs. Meeker then admitted to five prior structure fire losses, as well as various vehicle losses due to fires. The first structure fire occurred when their home in Dewitt, Iowa, burned and their personal property was destroyed. Two ceramic shop fires followed as well as, two mobile home fires in Missouri.

Following receipt of the investigatory materials, an attorney for Shelter, wrote to the Meekers advising them that Shelter was denying their claim.

In response, the Meekers sought damages for: dwelling coverage; personal property coverage; additional living expense coverage; removal of debris coverage; unlawful conspiracy; negligent conduct; other structures coverage; and coverage for loss of trees, shrubs, plants and lawns.

Prior to trial, the court dismissed a number of the Meekers complaints.

During trial, the Meekers denied that they had misrepresented the number of their prior fires. Barbara Meeker testified that when asked her about prior fire losses, she told the agent they had had "several," including the house in Iowa, the two ceramic shop fires, and the two mobile home fires in Missouri.

After evidence was heard at the jury trial, the court ruled that a legitimate inference could be drawn when coupling the agent's testimony regarding the Meekers' statements to him regarding prior fire losses with his testimony that he would not have issued the binder had he known of the prior fire losses.

The court entered judgment in favor of Shelter for $36,071.96 plus $13,149.22 interest for dwelling coverage, $37,130.19 plus $19,722.68 interest for property coverage, and $1,500 for additional living expenses.

In response, the Meekers alleged that the court overlooked, misinterpreted, or misstated material matters of law and fact in arriving at its opinion.

The court ruled the allegations and arguments, meritless and the motion for rehearing, or in the alternative to transfer to the Supreme Court, was denied.

MISREPRESENTATION

If any party to an insurance contract misstates a matter of fact, a **misrepresentation** has occurred. This can be grounds for **nullification** of the policy—or damages in excess of the policy limits.

An applicant who has been canceled by previous carriers for excessive claims and does not show this on the application is making a material misrepresentation, since the carrier would probably not issue a policy if this information was known. As in the case above, the contract can be voided by the company and any claim denied.

If you have an insurable loss, it is helpful to know the **duties required of you** as a policy owner. Generally, your policy states that you are required to:

- provide the insurance company with immediate written notice of a loss;

- notify law enforcement in case of loss by theft and a credit card fund transfer card company in case of loss to credit card or fund transfer card;

- protect your property from any further damage or make necessary repairs to protect the property;

- submit a complete and detailed inventory of all damaged and undamaged property, quantities, costs, ACV, and the amount of loss claimed;

- forward any legal papers received, such as a summons, to the company immediately;

- within 60 days of the loss, submit a signed proof of loss stating the time and origin of loss, interest of all parties involved, other insurance, value of each item, and any other information which the policy requires.

Your insurance company may also request that you submit appropriate records, exhibit the remains of the damaged property, or submit to examinations under oath.

If you don't comply with your duties after a loss occurs, your insurance company will not be obligated to pay your loss.

Contacting your insurer and the police after you have suffered a loss is a relatively important part of the claims process and fairly simple. But in addition to complying with your duties after a loss—you want to do them in a way that will assure you the maximum timely settlement. And knowing how your insurance company looks at a claim will help you with this process.

> In order to get recovery for losses covered by your policy, promptly notify your insurer should a loss occur.

You have 20 days to provide **notice of a claim** to your insurer or agent. If for some reason you can't make this time frame after an accidental injury, you must send notice of a claim as soon as reasonably possible.

> Don't throw anything out after a loss has occurred, an adjuster may want to see all the damaged items before approving your claim.

If a loss covered under your policy causes damage in such a way as to expose your property to any further damage, you have an obligation to make **reasonable repairs** or to take other steps to protect the property.

For example: If a windstorm blows away a portion of your roof, the policy would pay for—and actually require— temporary repairs to the roof to avoid further damage to the interior of the structure. If you don't make the reasonable repairs, the policy won't cover any further damage.

A standard policy allows you to move your property from a premises threatened by a covered peril to a safe place for a period of 30 days. Coverage would apply to the property for moving and while at the other location for loss from any cause—which expands your coverage considerably.

However, if you don't take these precautions, your insurance company may interpret that as a failure to reasonably protect your property from damage.

If your insurer is looking for a way to get out of paying a claim, it may try to expand a dispute over prevention into a dispute over **policy owner neglect**—a specifically excluded coverage.

Disputes between you and your company generally center around coverage issues—specifically, whether or not a loss is covered under your policy. Because companies protect themselves from the negative financial impact of paying out large claims, they often deny coverage by pointing at some fundamental issue—often something not related to the specifics of the claim. This is why it is so important to know your duties as a policy holder after a loss occurs.

LIMIT OF LIABILITY

When a covered loss occurs, your insurer has a **limit of liability**, or legal responsibility to honor their contractual agreement to pay damages to you or to a third party on your behalf.

The limit of liability is simply the amount of coverage, the maximum amount of insurance or upper limit that the insurance company is legally obligated to pay if a covered loss occurs.

If a covered loss occurs for less than the limit of liability, your insurance company will pay the amount of the loss (minus any deductible that may apply). If the amount of the covered loss is more than the limit of liability, your insurance company will pay the limit of its coverage and you will be responsible for paying the additional costs.

PROOF OF LOSS

It is important to document your loss as thoroughly as possible. After contacting your insurer, they will usually send you a **proof of loss form** to complete.

In some cases, they may send an adjuster out to your house to go over the form with you. By having an inventory ahead of time, filling out this form will be a lot easier.

A proof of loss form generally tends to have uniformity with different insurance companies. If you're aren't sure what should go into this report, here are a few guidelines on what should be included:

- the time and cause of the loss;
- specifications of damage and detailed repair estimates;

- any damaged personal property;

- any other insurance which may apply;

- the interest of you and all other parties in the property involved (such as mortgage companies, lien holders, etc.);

- changes in the title or occupancy of the property during the term policy;

- if possible, receipts for any property that has been damaged;

- evidence or affidavit that supports a claim under the Credit Card, Fund Transfer Card, Forgery and Counterfeit Money coverage, stating the amount and cause of loss.

Losses will be adjusted and paid to you— unless the policy indicates that payment should be made to someone else, such as a mortgage holder.

It's a good idea to **make a list** of everything that's been stolen or damaged as soon as possible. Include a **description of each item, the date of purchase, and what it would cost to replace today** (If you have replacement-cost coverage). Any receipts, bills, photographs, or serial numbers from high-ticket purchases can also be helpful in establishing the value of your losses.

You don't have to wait for a major loss to occur to do this. You should keep a list that includes this information in a safe place at all times.

ABANDONMENT

An **abandonment clause** prohibits you from abandoning your property to your insurer in order to claim a total loss.

Although the company may choose to acquire the damaged property which can be sold for salvage and may choose to pay a total loss, you cannot insist that your insurance company take possession of any property.

For example: You have a loss due to a fire in the storage shed in your backyard. Most of its contents are damaged, but there are some that are not. You can not tell your insurance company , "I had $6,000 worth of stuff in the shed. Pay me $6,000 and the stuff is yours." Your insurer will usually not accept this kind of a proposition because it has to make arrangements for hauling, repair, and sale of the salvageable property and it usually does not care to do this.

If you collected on a property loss due to a theft and the property is recovered two months later, you have the option to take the property and pay your insurer the original amount paid for the loss. Or you can keep the money and let the company keep the property.

If property that has been stolen and paid for by the insurance company is **recovered** later on, you can elect to take the property and pay back the insurance company the amount it originally paid for the loss. An alternative is to keep the money and let the company keep the property.

Despite the specified amount of insurance, your **insurable interest** may limit the amount paid on a claim. Other parties may have an insurable interest in your property as an owner, mortgage holder, vendor, lien holder, stockholder, joint owner, bailee, or lease holder.

Once an insurance company has paid you for the loss you sustained, it acquires your rights in the claim. This transfer is called **subrogation**.

> **Example:** Your neighbor loses control of his car and crashes into your garage. Your insurance company, after paying you, now has the right to sue your neighbor to collect from him the amount it paid to you. Once you receive payment, you "subrogate," or pass on, your rights in the claim to the insurance company.

If you become **bankrupt or insolvent**, the company remains obliged to provide coverage and to respond to the terms and conditions of the policy.

Your homeowners policy may include the following language: "With respect to the personal liability coverage, this policy is excess over any other valid and collectible insurance."

The practical application of this clause varies, depending on the other insurance. Duplication of coverage often ends up with both insurance companies **contributing to payment** of a loss.

> The other insurance clause doesn't apply to so-called true excess liability insurance—like standard umbrella liability policies. Umbrella policies remain a secondary form of insurance to a homeowners policy.
>
> Once your insurer has paid you for the loss you sustained, it has the rights in the claim. This transfer is called **subrogation.**

For example: Your neighbor loses control of his car and crashes into your garage and its contents. Your insurance company, after paying you, now has the right to sue your neighbor to collect from him the amount it paid top you.

Once you receive payment, you "subrogate," or pass on, your rights in the claim to the insurance company.

If your insurer fails to provide you with **claims forms** within 15 days after receiving your notice of claims, you may comply with the policy's proof of loss requirements by writing to your insurance company and detailing the occurrence, and the character and extent of the loss.

Millions of insureds often slip up on their insurance coverage— later to find out that the new $2,000 computer that they brought home isn't covered when stolen three weeks later.

Don't wait till you get home from the store to purchase coverage. Chances are, you'll know ahead of time that you are going to make a purchase of that size. Insure it first—then bring it home.

Most people know that they need to insure their possessions, but they often get careless when it comes down to purchasing coverage. At times, they often leave out items or don't purchase the right amount of coverage. One way too help avoid this is to videotaping everything you own.

Appraisers are now suggesting that you simply walk through your residence with a video camera and tape everything. Film the paintings on your walls, your jewelry box, and even your closet. Most people remember to insure their jewelry and their mink coat but forget to appraise their wardrobe, which could be as much as $50,000.

If you have a videotape, photos or the actual appraisal written down—be sure to make a hard copy of it and keep it of the insured premises.

People often go through all the trouble of paying for an appraisal, taking photos, or videotaping only to leave this evidence on the insured premises.

This won't help if your house burns down and takes the appraisal with it.

If your list is on a computer program, or you have receipts, appraisals, photos or tapes, be sure that they are kept safely off the premises. A good suggestion is to keep these items in a safety-deposit box or inside a vault off the insured premises.

LOSS PAYABLE CLAUSE

The **loss payable clause** of a standard policy, states that if you provide the proof of loss and other information—and the amount of loss has been agreed upon—your insurer will pay for the loss **within 60 days** (laws may vary with this time limit in each state).

> Your duty as a policyholder is to **assist the insurance company** in making settlements, making claims against other parties who might be responsible for the loss, be available for court trials, hearings, or suits, and give evidence as required.

If you don't provide proof of loss information, or in some way alter the information, you may find yourself shelling money out of your own pocket for repairs or even replacements.

However, there is a **time limit** on certain defenses. This limits the period in which your company may try to deny coverage by questioning the truthfulness of your statements on an insurance application. Depending on the state in which you live, this law will vary from either a two- or three-year period.

After your policy has been in effect for the specified number of years, your insurer can no longer contest coverage on the basis of your omissions or misrepresentations unless your insurance company can prove that they were made with the intent to defraud. This provision is also called the **incontestable provision**.

If you have provided the necessary proof of loss forms and the actual amount of the loss has been agreed upon by both you and your insurer, your insurance company will have 60 days to pay out your claim. Even if you are angry because your property has been stolen, you can't change the black and white of the policy.

In the 1992 Illinois appeals court decision *John Mazur v. Dena Hunt, Crum and Forster and United States Fire Insurance Co.*, a policyholder's impatience worsened his loss.

Thieves broke into John Mazur's home and stole several pieces of jewelry. U.S. Fire paid him for some of the jewelry taken—items for which he had signed a proof of loss report.

However, U.S. Fire refused to pay for the loss of two additional pieces which were not included on the proof of loss form. Mazur sued U.S. Fire and its agents for not covering those two pieces, which he claimed were worth $41,000.

He alleged breach by U.S. Fire and Crum and Forster of the "newly acquired property" provisions of his insurance policy. Under these provisions, U.S. Fire was required to pay the lesser of "25 percent of the amount of insurance for that class of property" or $10,000.

For these alleged violations, Mazur sought compensatory damages of $10,000, costs, pre-judgment interest and attorneys fees.

He also alleged that the jewelry at issue was fully covered under the policy. On this count, he charged U.S. Fire with breaching the policy and sought compensatory damages for the full value of the jewelry, $41,000, plus costs, pre-judgment interest and attorney fees.

Finally, he charged Crum and Forster insurance agent Dena Hunt with fraud. He claimed she used the proof of loss report to bar his claim for the two pieces of jewelry that were omitted.

According to his complaint, Mazur signed the loss report because Hunt said it would not bar his subsequent claim for the two recently-acquired pieces.

He said she said by signing right away, he could get some of the money and not lose his right to claim the two additional items of jewelry at a later time.

For this alleged misrepresentation, Mazur wanted compensatory damages of $41,000 and punitive damages of $2 million.

U.S. Fire and Crum and Forster answered that the proof of loss form had been "executed by the plaintiff in full satisfaction and indemnity for all claims and demands upon the insurance company issuing the Insurance Policy in question."

They argued that the final fraud charge should be rejected because Illinois insurance law provided administrative remedies for coverage disputes.

The trial court sided with the insurance company and agent. It rejected Mazur's lawsuit. He appealed.

The appellate court didn't buy his argument any more than the lower court did. It ruled held that Mazurs' claim for fraud against insurer and agent based on alleged negligent misrepresentations was preempted by the Insurance Code.

"Although labeled as a fraud count, the issue in [this case] is the amount of loss payable under the policy, with allegations that defendant's failure to pay is unreasonable or vexatious, a claim which is preempted" by the insurance code, the court wrote. "Apart from not being paid for the two pieces of jewelry, [Mazur] has not alleged that he suffered any additional harm from defendants' conduct."

Also, it is important to maintain an adequate level of insurance-to-value. Even when replacement cost coverage applies, the final amount may not exceed the amount that you actually spent to replace the property, or the policy limit for the damaged property.

If you don't agree with your insurance company about the value of a loss, your method of appeal is outlined by the standard policy. The insurance company states:

> *If you and we fail to agree on the amount of loss, either may demand an appraisal of the loss. In this event, each party will choose a competent appraiser within 20*

days after receiving a written request from the other. The two appraisers will choose an umpire. If they cannot agree upon an umpire within 15 days, you or we may request that the choice be made by a judge of a court of record in the state where the [house] is located. The appraisers will separately set the amount of loss. If the appraisers submit a written report of an agreement to us, the amount agreed upon will be the amount of loss. If they fail to agree, they will submit their differences to the umpire. A decision agreed to by any two will set the amount of loss.

From time to time, policy owners bring suits against their insurance companies when they are dissatisfied over claim adjustments. Before this can be done, you must comply with the **policy provisions** concerning the reporting of the loss, cooperating with the company in settling the loss, etc.—and any suit must be brought **within one year** after the loss.

Be sure to update your insurance coverage. Many people forget to update their coverage beyond the automatic inflation of most policies.

Whenever language in an insurance policy is ambiguous, any dispute over coverage is ruled in favor of the policy owner. The insurance company has its opportunity to set terms in the drafting of the policy.

PROPERTY VALUATION

Property losses under the basic homeowners or dwelling form are generally settled on an **actual cash value basis**. All forms support the principle of **indemnity**, which—in this context—means recovery may not exceed the smallest of four amounts:

- the ACV of the property at the time of loss,

- the policy limit for the coverage,

- the amount necessary to repair or replace the property,

- the amount reflecting the insured's interest in the property at the time of the loss.

When a loss is adjusted on an actual cash value basis, a deduction is made by the insurance company for the **depreciation** of the property. The term depreciation refers to the gradual reduction in the value of property as a result of time and use.

If you are looking to insure your possessions under a homeowners policy, make sure that you insure the contents for the maximum amount. If you don't, when you file a claim you may find that your insurance company insures personal property for only 50 percent of your home's insurance.

For example, you would only get $100,000 towards your personal property if your home was insured for $200,000. However, if you find out ahead of time, you may want to purchase more insurance or a floater scheduling valuables separately.

If you have personal property that is not scheduled on your homeowners policy, it should be insured with the more expensive, **replacement cost** coverage so that if a loss occurs, you can replace it rather than receiving only the actual cash value (ACV) you paid for it. (ACV coverage ill take depreciation into consideration giving you only a percentage of what the item's cost was when you purchased it based on the years you have owned it.

The final recovery may not exceed the amount actually spent to repair or replace the property or the policy limit for the damages.

If after meeting with an adjuster, you and your insurance company fail to agree on the value of your loss, your method of appeal is outlined by the standard homeowners policy. The policy states:

> *If you and we fail to agree on the amount of loss, either may demand an appraisal of the loss. In this event, each party will choose a competent appraiser within 20 days after receiving a request fro the other. The two appraisers will choose an umpire. If they cannot agree upon an umpire within 15 days, you or we may request that the choice be made by a judge of a court of record in the state where the [house] is located. The appraisers will separately set the amount of loss. If the appraisers submit a written report of an agreement to us, the amount agreed upon will be the amount of the loss. If they fail to agree, they will submit their differences to the umpire. A deci-*

> *sion agreed to by any two will set the
> amount of the loss.*

If you are worried about the valuation of the things you have lost, find an appraiser who belongs to the American Society of Appraisers in Washington or the Appraisers Association of America in New York. Both groups can provide you with a directory of members: the American Society of Appraisers, P.O. Box 17265, Washington, D.C. 20041, (703)478-2228 ($10); or the Appraisers Association of America, 386 Park Ave., Suite 2000, New York, N.Y. 10016, (212)889-5405 ($14.95).

You can also get recommendations on appraisers by calling the Appraisal Institute in Chicago, IL (312)335-4100 or the National Association of Realtors in Chicago, IL (312)329-8200.

Some other points to remember about claims for personal property:

- When there is a loss to a pair or a set, the insurance company has the right to restore or replace any part of the pair or set in order to restore its value, or to pay the difference between the ACV of the property before and after the loss.

- Supporting evidence is required for losses insured by the credit card, fund transfer, forgery and counterfeit money coverage and, in the case of a credit card or fund transfer loss, the insured must notify the appropriate card company.

- Coverage for personal property usually kept at an insured's residence other than the residence premises is limited to the larger of $1,000 or 10 percent of the standard personal property limit. But if personal property is moved to a newly acquired principal residence, this limitation does not apply during the first 30 days after the property is moved.

OTHER DWELLING AND PROPERTY CLAIMS ISSUES

In most cases, insurance companies generally settle claims by **making payments** to you, the policy owner. However, your insurer also has the option of **repairing or replacing the damaged property**. This will occur when replacement can be made at a cost to the company which is less than that which the insured could negotiate.

The **pair and set clause** in the standard policy recognizes that the loss of one item from a pair or set may reduce the value of a pair or set by **an amount greater than the physical proportion** of the lost item to the set. It usually comes into play when items of jewelry, fine arts or antiques are involved.

Example: A pair of antique candelabra is valued at $3,000. One of the sticks is stolen in a burglary. The value of the one remaining is established at $1,200—so the value lost is $1,800. This

---

would be the amount of the loss. If the missing candelabra could be replaced for $1,700, then the company has the option of making the replacement.

STRENGTHENING CLAIMS

Be sure to read your policy. This is very important. If you know what kind of coverage you have, you are more than likely to receive all that you are entitled to. The following is a list of common practices that help to support claims:

- **Keep careful records**. Make copies of everything. It's also a good idea to take notes at any meetings and conversations you have with your agent, insurer, or claims adjuster.

- **Verify the adjuster's estimate**. Don't accept an estimate without getting a written bid from another contractor.

- **Don't settle for an unfair settlement**. If you can't reach an agreement with your adjuster, contact your agent or the insurer's claim-department manager.

  If you're still dissatisfied, some state insurance departments offer mediation services. In addition, most policies allow for an independent appraisal or arbitration process to resolve disputes over money. That decision is usually binding.

Keep track of when your premium is due and the

expiration date of your policy. If you're late paying a renewal you may find yourself in a lot of trouble.

> The easiest way for an insurance company to deny a claim is to show that the policy was not in effect when the loss occurred.

Of course, the issues aren't always so clear. If a loss occurs **just before the expiration date** of the policy and **continues** for two months afterward, the loss would be fully covered.

However, a dispute could arise over when—exactly—the loss first occurred.

> Example: You make a claim that, because of an insured flaw in the construction of your house, a series of accidents began during a policy's coverage period and has continued afterward. The company may have to pay for damage which happened after the policy term.
> If the insurance company can show that the loss didn't begin and continue—but is, in fact, several losses occurring independently—it can limit its liability to claims that relate to accidents that occurred during the policy period.

CONCLUSION

If you have chosen your insurance effectively, making a claim will be pretty straightforward. Of course, the circumstances leading up to a claim (burglary, fire or other disasters) can make even the calmest mind nervous and edgy.

This chapter has focused on the effective measures to take with regard to a claim—from reporting an accident to choosing the right claim adjuster.

This *book* has attempted to give you a basic understanding of the insurance that covers your valuable possessions. This is complicated coverage...much more so than homeowners or car insurance.

Your valuables may be as simple as a nice stamp collection or as complex as tens of thousands of dollars in somewhat business-related electronic equipment.

The insurance you need for this stuff is a mixed bag of stand-alone policies and smaller add-ons. Good luck sorting through it.

HOW TO MAKE A CLAIM

INDEX

abandonment 204

actual cash value 17, 25, 64, 67, 77, 84-88, 113, 121, 134, 158, 213-214

additional living expense 22, 31, 175, 198

additions and alterations 40, 73

all-risk coverage 55, 95, 185

American Society of Appraisers 215

appraisal 77, 81-82, 207-208, 212, 214-215, 218

Appraisal Institute 215

Appraisers Association of America 215

audio 61-64

auto 139-143, 148, 186, 193, 195, 213

auto insurance 1, 6, 13, 57-59, 66, 97-98

bicycle 79, 81, 127-128, 140

boats 1, 27, 51, 75, 79, 83, 96, 102-103, 107, 128, 147-149, 187

broad form perils 42, 113

broad homeowners policy 24

broad theft coverage 41, 44, 52, 54, 162-163, 170, 174

business loss exposure 6

business or professional equipment 75

business personal property 4-5

cameras 13, 15, 59, 73-74, 78, 81, 83-84, 114-115, 123, 128

cellular phones 13

change of endorsement 63

co-op and condominium coverage 25

coin and stamp collection 90

collections 74, 81, 86, 89-90, 115, 118-121, 132, 160
collision 58-59, 65-66, 134, 144, 149, 151
collision damage waiver 65-66
computers 6, 13, 18, 28, 60-61, 66, 74, 124, 126, 160, 187
Condominium Insurance Specialists 38
contents 4, 6, 21, 24-25, 40-42, 54, 58, 111, 182, 189, 196, 204, 206, 214
contents broad form 41
conventions 129, 132
covered perils 117, 124, 131
credit card 32-35, 52
custom and after market coverage 64
customized insurance 14, 16
debris removal 31-33, 187-188
duties after a loss 199-200
dwelling 162-164, 170, 174-176, 178-180, 182, 186-188, 190, 192, 197-198, 213, 216
dwelling contents 4
dwelling coverage 13, 22, 30
electronic data processing 16, 123
equity value 8
fair rental value 31
fine art 81, 83, 85-86, 91, 114, 117-118, 120-122, 133, 192, 217
fragile articles 74, 76, 118, 133
full replacement 18, 158
furs 4, 15, 26, 50, 54, 71, 76, 80-81, 83-84, 111, 115, 123, 160, 166
golf equipment 81, 83, 116, 119
guaranteed replacement-cost 24
high-value property 4, 66, 74
homeowners insurance 1, 6, 21-22, 24, 29, 33, 36, 39, 131, 147-149, 153, 162, 176-178

homeowners policy 111, 113-115, 124-125, 137, 141, 144-145, 185-187, 196, 206, 214

individual articles floater 80

inland marine 15-16, 110-116, 117, 119, 122, 125, 127-128, 178, 186, 192

inland marine insurance 15, 69, 110

insurable net worth 8

Insurance Services Office 124

insured 3, 7, 9, 15-17, 23, 28-29, 32-35, 37, 42, 44-45, 47-54, 59, 67, 73-75, 79, 83, 85-89, 91, 94-95, 97-99, 101-107, 110, 112-115, 117-123, 125-127, 129, 134, 142-143, 145, 148-152, 156, 159, 163, 167-168, 174-175, 178, 179-186, 188-191, 193, 207-208, 213-214, 216, 219

intrinsic value 4-5

jewelry 4-5, 8, 15, 26-27, 39, 50, 54, 66, 70-71, 74, 76, 80-81, 83-84, 111, 114-116, 122-123, 153, 157, 159-160, 162, 166, 207, 209-211, 217

landlord 2, 25, 35, 37-38, 40, 43, 55, 100, 188

leasehold improvement 40

legal liability 40, 104, 138

liability coverage 3, 6-7, 12, 22-23, 25, 30, 58, 93, 103, 107, 109, 144, 149-150, 178-179, 188, 206

limits of liability 26, 49, 151, 191

loss 1-3, 6, 8, 9, 15-17, 19, 22, 26-28, 31-35, 38, 40-44, 48-49, 51, 53-54, 57-58, 62-64, 66-67, 93-95, 98, 101, 104-106, 108-110, 113-114, 118-124, 127-128, 133-136, 138-139, 141-142, 146-148, 150-152, 156-158, 161, 163-166, 168, 170-171, 174-178, 182-185, 187-193, 195-219

loss of use 30-31, 101

loss settlement 87, 120, 146, 158

loss to a pair 85-87, 121, 134, 215

mechanical breakdown 124, 126, 128

misrepresentation 196, 198, 209, 211
mobile home coverage 145
mobile property 4, 6
motor vehicles 4, 6, 23, 52, 75, 97, 112
multi-peril policy 55
musical instruments 13, 15, 73-74, 81, 83-85, 116,
    160
National Association of Insurance Commissioners
    (NAIC) 113
named perils 24-25, 43, 74, 91, 114, 152, 184, 188
negligence liability 41
newly acquired property 84, 126, 129, 210
occurrence 93, 95, 97, 99, 105, 109-110, 181, 183,
    207
off-premises theft 50
on-premises theft 171
participating policies 126
pension benefits 8
personal articles floater 82-85, 87, 90-91, 185
personal auto policy 98, 55, 57, 61-62, 143, 186
personal effects 66
personal effects floater 122
personal injury coverage 99
personal property coverage 30
personal-effects coverage 66
pet 118-119, 138, 142, 157, 167, 212, 214
portable property 74
principal residence 31, 51, 165, 216
professional liability 109, 181
property 3-9, 12-19, 21-23, 25-27, 29-33, 36, 38-44,
    48-55, 58-60, 63-64, 66-71, 73-91, 96-101, 105-
    106, 108, 111-115, 117-126, 128, 129, 132-134, 139-
    140, 143, 145-149, 151, 153, 158, 161-166, 170-
    171, 173-192, 197-201, 203-205, 209-210, 212-216

property coverage 113, 120, 146-147, 149, 153, 162, 170, 175-176, 187, 197-198

property damage 9, 31, 60, 87, 96-98, 101, 106, 108, 148, 151, 187

property loss 3, 16, 139, 204, 213

radar detectors 14, 62

real property 3, 12, 22, 101, 182, 187

rental car 65

renters policy 13, 24, 36, 40-41, 45, 48, 51, 89, 93, 158, 188

replacement cost 17, 25, 121, 146, 158, 188-189, 211, 214

residence employee 31, 45, 48, 51-52, 164, 174

residence premises 27-31, 33, 71-72, 78, 105, 148, 179, 190, 216

scheduled personal property 74, 83-84, 90, 115, 118, 120, 146, 185, 192

silverware 4, 15, 26-27, 49-50, 71, 73, 81, 83, 116, 165-166

sound reproduction 60-61

special coverage 112, 131, 145-146, 179, 185

special homeowners policy 24

special limits of liability 49

specialty or customized policies 16

sports equipment 4, 13, 18, 49, 73-74, 78, 90, 115, 153, 160

sports memorabilia 115

spouse 47, 78, 152, 180

sub-limits of liability 49

tenants insurance 41

theft coverage 41, 44, 50, 52-55, 148, 162-163, 170-171, 174

trip cancellation 135

trip transit floater 89

umbrella liability 7, 96
umbrella policy 7, 15, 94, 96, 98-99, 102-103, 105-
    110, 192-193
unique objects 74
unlawful acts 106
unscheduled property 74
valuation 113, 120, 146, 213, 215
vandalism 3, 33, 44, 54, 76
watercraft 4, 6, 26, 49, 50, 71, 97, 103, 106, 147-153,
    165-166
wedding 89, 114, 116, 137, 138
Western Insurance Information Service (WIIS) 38-
    39